The Underground Stations
of Leslie Green

David Leboff

Capital Transport

I wish to thank the following people who have assisted me during the preparation of this book:
– My colleagues at London Underground: Nick Bailey, Ian Docwra, Ron Grant and Colin Williams;
– Sheila Taylor and her colleagues at London's Transport Museum;
– Teresa Doherty at Transport *for* London Archives & Record Management;
– Staff at the London Metropolitan Archive, RIBA Library and the Westminster Reference Library;
– David Lawrence, Doug Rose, Mike Stollery and Mike Ashworth for their proof-reading and constructive criticism;
– And of course, my wife Sara for her support and stoicism over the months!

I am keen to hear from readers with information or queries about Leslie Green or his stations. I may be contacted via Capital Transport Publishing or by using email at the following address:
david.leboff@btinternet.com

For my beloved children Savanna and Daniel.

Colour photography:
James Whiting, David Leboff

Black and white photography:
London's Transport Museum

ISBN 185414 255 0
Published by Capital Transport Publishing, 38 Long Elmes, Harrow Weald, Middlesex
Designed by Tim Demuth
Printed by CS Graphics, Singapore
© David Leboff 2002

Contents

Abbreviations

BPCR	Brompton & Piccadilly Circus Railway
BSWR	Baker Street & Waterloo Railway (now part of the Bakerloo Line)
CCEHR	Charing Cross, Euston & Hampstead Railway (now part of the Northern Line)
GNPBR	Great Northern, Piccadilly & Brompton Railway (now part of the Piccadilly Line)
GNSR	Great Northern & Strand Railway
RIBA	Royal Institute of British Architects
UERL	Underground Electric Railways Company of London Ltd
UTS	Underground Ticketing System – a 1980s programme to install new ticket offices and passenger operated machines at every station, with automatic gates at central London locations

Glossary of architectural terms

Cartouche: decorative architectural feature resembling a scroll and derived from a classical design.

Cornice: horizontal moulded projection, which crowns a wall, building or arch.

Dado: lower portion of interior wall when decorated differently from the upper part.

Faience: glazed earthenware, fashionably used at the turn of the 19th/20th century as a hard-wearing decorative external cladding.

Keystone: central locking stone in an arch or portal.

Mullion: vertical member dividing panes within a window.

Pediment: triangular or curved upper part crowning a window or the front of a building.

Pilaster: rectangular column in the shape of a pillar projecting from a wall.

Portal: gateway or doorway, especially a large or elaborate version.

Render: cementitious coating applied as a weatherproof cover to a brick or blockwork wall.

Roundel: symbol representing London Underground / Transport and one of the world's most distinctive pieces of corporate identity. Has undergone many changes since first used on stations around 1910 in the form of a blue bar on a red disc.

Soffit: ceiling or underside of an architectural feature.

Stretcher bond: pattern of rectangular bricks or tiles laid horizontally with alternate courses moved along by half a unit.

Terracotta: unglazed, typically brownish-red earthenware, often used for moulded decoration on buildings.

Transom: horizontal member dividing panes within a window.

Voussoir: one of the radiating wedge-shaped blocks forming the upper part of an arch.

Changes of station name

Current name	Previous names
Aldwych	Strand
Archway	Highgate; Archway (Highgate); Highgate (Archway)
Arsenal	Gillespie Road
Charing Cross (Bakerloo)	Trafalgar Square
Charing Cross (Northern)	Charing Cross (Strand); Strand
Embankment	Charing Cross (Embankment); Charing Cross
Goodge Street	Tottenham Court Road
Green Park	Dover Street
King's Cross St Pancras	King's Cross; King's Cross for St Pancras
Lambeth North	Kennington Road; Westminster Bridge Road, Lambeth (North)
Marylebone	Great Central
Tottenham Court Road	Oxford Street
Warren Street	Euston Road

Preface

THE STATIONS designed by Leslie Green are perhaps the most under-rated of all those built for the railway companies that now constitute London's Underground system. Later architects such as Charles Clark and in particular Charles Holden have taken the limelight and this is perhaps reflected in the fact that only three of Green's buildings (Gloucester Road, Holloway Road and Mornington Crescent) have statutory listed status compared to 18 designed solely by Holden and his office. Whilst acknowledging the architectural excellence of the latter, such an incongruity seems unwarranted.

Green's work has made a substantial impact on the urban 'landscape' of our capital city for two primary reasons. Firstly, there is the sheer number of the station buildings he designed – forty or so, of which around two thirds have survived almost a century of bombing, reconstruction and redevelopment. Secondly, he adopted a simple style that was used in almost modular form to suit the wide variety of locations where the stations were sited. The deployment of ox-blood red faience as a cladding material may not have been to everyone's taste over the decades but it meant that these buildings were clearly identifiable as tube stations – a fact reflected in their depiction outside the real world in situations as diverse as the Smithsonian Institute in Washington DC and the set of Eastenders!

As well as giving some background to Leslie Green himself, this book provides a photographic record of his buildings and their internal finishes and fittings which may still be seen by the general public as they travel around the Underground network. Whilst reference may be made to later additions, the primary concentration is on original features which survive, some of which may not be obvious to the casual observer. As a result, only passing reference has been made to station buildings which are now disused or have since been demolished – the former in particular having been described at length in recent publications.

I hope that this book will act as an inspiration to users of the Underground, especially to those who travel through Green's stations on a regular basis, so that they are able to gain a sense of the architecture and history around them.

David Leboff
Stanmore, Middlesex
July 2002

The man and his buildings

Leslie Green (1875–1908).
Copyright: the estate of Vera Stubbs.
Source: London's Transport Museum

LESLIE WILLIAM GREEN was born on 6 February 1875 at 99 Portsdown Road (now Randolph Avenue) in the salubrious surroundings of Maida Vale, at that time a small suburb off the Edgware Road north of Paddington. The eldest of four children, he was brought up in comfortable surroundings by his parents Arthur William Green and Emily Ann Green. From the age of 13, he was educated at Dover College, passing his Preliminary Examination in November 1891.

The early years

From an early age Green demonstrated his interest in architecture by following in the footsteps of his father. Soon after completing his exams, he joined his father's practice in Suffolk Street off Pall Mall as an apprentice. For one year from summer 1893, he attended the South Kensington School of Art to further his education and he then studied at a college in Paris for a further year. It was during this latter period that he first encountered the emerging decorative style that had become known as 'Art Nouveau' – a style which was amongst other things marked by the use of sinuous lines and stylised flowers. This experience was to remain with young Leslie and was to influence much of his subsequent work.

In late 1895, Green returned to London and returned to his father's practice. By this time, he had been promoted to be Arthur's assistant and it was in this role that he was involved in the design and execution of several buildings in central London including a large block of flats in Buckingham Palace Road and the Pall Mall Safe Deposit at 10 St Alban's Street.

Green however was not content to work in Arthur's shadow for long and in 1897, he decided to enter practice under his own name,

with offices at 11 Suffolk Street, apparently sharing offices with his father. In November of the same year, he qualified for studentship at the Royal Institute of British Architects, passing the examinations for associate membership of the RIBA in 1898 and being elected a full member on 6 March the following year. In early 1900, the practice moved to 19 Haymarket and again to Adelphi House at 71 Strand at its junction with Adam Street three years later. In 1903, he became a member of the Architectural Association – an organisation which then as now aimed to promote and afford facilities for the study of architecture.

For six years after commencing in private practice, Green worked on a wide variety of projects, although none were of major significance. Examples included the remodelling of the interiors of properties in Kensington Palace Gardens, Portland Place and Sussex Square, along with various alterations and additions to Messrs Lewis & Allenby's retail premises (since rebuilt) at 193–197 Regent Street.

The Underground beckons . . .

Green's formative years as an architect coincided with a massive period of interest in underground railways, especially in London. The opening of the world's first deep-tube railway, the City & South London, in December 1890 generated considerable speculative development by entrepreneurs eager to cash in on the new technology. Amongst those railway schemes for which parliamentary powers were forthcoming were the Baker Street & Waterloo, the Brompton & Piccadilly Circus, the Great Northern & Strand and the Charing Cross Euston & Hampstead. Although construction had commenced on the first of these in 1898, a shortage of funding led to activities being suspended in 1901. Meanwhile, work on the other three lines had not begun for similar reasons.

This sorry state of affairs was redeemed with the arrival of Charles Tyson Yerkes, an American financier who had revolutionised urban transport systems in several major US cities during the late 1890s. One by one, the four lines, along with the District Railway and other operators, were bought up and eventually incorporated into a single firm, the Underground Electric Railways Company of London Ltd (UERL), in April 1902. The resultant injection of capital led to rapid progress of all four schemes, although two – the BPCR and GNSR – were soon merged to form the Great Northern Piccadilly & Brompton Railway.

A watercolour from 1906 depicting Oxford Circus station, painted by and signed by Green himself.

One key consequence of this merger was a high level of standardisation of many aspects of the railways' design and operation. Perhaps the most evident manifestation of this was the stations, which were intended to have a certain uniformity of appearance. In September 1903, Leslie Green's life changed for ever when he was appointed by the UERL to act as the architect in charge of station design for the three tube railways, working alongside Harry Wharton Ford, the District Railway's staff architect. For this mammoth responsibility, his practice was to be paid £2,000 per annum plus office expenses. A particular point of interest relates to the exact terms of his commission i.e. 'to act as Architect . . . for the station buildings *above the ground level*' [author's italics], indicating that Green would have little if any influence over the appearance of the subterranean areas.

It should be noted that three of the stations served by the GNPBR were not covered by Green's brief – Finsbury Park being built by the Great Northern Railway (under whose platforms the new line was constructed), while

Hammersmith and Barons Court were redesigned by the District Railway under Ford's direction.

Station design

There was little time for Green to waste, for work had already commenced on all three of the new railways. His task was to develop a style of building that could be adapted for use according to the individual site constraints, whilst at the same time presenting a consistent and attractive appearance. Such an intention was not unique to these Yerkes Tubes, as they were to become known, for both the earlier main deep level railways in the capital – the City & South London and the Central London – employed a similar philosophy, with buildings designed by T Phillips Figgis and Harry Measures respectively. However, Green's solution was more radical and flexible.

In essence, his buildings were constructed around a load-bearing steel frame, upon which brickwork and then ox-blood red glazed faience

The Euston station building shortly after its opening in 1907, showing the CCEHR style of lettering, together with the later additions of the Underground logo on one of the fascias and also in illuminated vertical form. A photograph of this building today appears on page 76.

cladding was applied. Green used the latter material because of the relative speed and low expense entailed with its manufacture (by the Leeds Fireclay Company at a price of nine shillings per superficial foot!), especially where decorative mouldings were incorporated within the design. All of the stations with street level buildings, with the exception of Great Central

(later Marylebone) and Waterloo, had two storeys, with the vast majority having lift machine equipment on the upper floor, crowned by a cornice. Each was divided into a series of bays, with semi-circular windows above and shops or access portals into the station interior below. Lettering was applied to upper and/or lower friezes to indicate the station and railway names, while Maxim arc lamps on ornate brackets illuminated the façades. The robust nature of the metal structure, supplied by Fulham Steelworks Ltd, allowed for the later addition of extra floors should they prove to be commercially viable. This was a typical feature of American buildings and perhaps reflected Yerkes's influence.

Whilst almost all of Green's stations followed this basic format (exceptions included Tottenham Court Road [now Goodge Street] and Regent's Park, which had no surface structures), there was considerable variation between the buildings in the detail and the way in which the format was applied to particular circumstances. The majority had a single straight frontage but some stations had two or even three façades – mostly connected in some way, but in a handful of cases completely separate from each other. The glazed arches were interspersed with small round or rectangular windows, the layout being different at every site. In most cases, the façades were fairly plain and lacking in decorative detail, other than ornate carving to the underside of the round window 'hoods' and various cartouche features (the designs of which were unique to each station). The most prominent exception to this was the Brompton Road elevation to Knightsbridge station, which

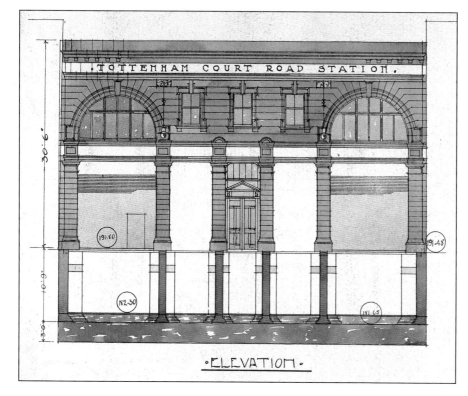

featured extensive Art Nouveau floral designs moulded onto the faience either side of each arched window. Note should also be made of Holborn, where granite was used instead of the usual faience.

The most prominent difference between the buildings constructed for the three railways was the nature of the lettering. The BSWR stations included the station name in raised gilded lettering on the lower frieze, with the company name spelt out in metal characters applied to the faience upper frieze. A similar format was followed for the majority of GNPBR stations, although the metal letters were omitted and the railway name often included (as initials) on the lower frieze instead. In contrast, the CCEHR buildings transposed the station and company names and made use of block letters in black on a white tiled background. There were several exceptions to this general arrangement on the GNPBR which followed the CCEHR pattern, the common factor being that most of the buildings were completed in 1907 after the opening of the railway, by which time the contractors were perhaps encouraged to introduce cost savings.

The interior of the ticket halls again followed a standard format. In the vast majority of cases, the walls were clad in deep green tiling, topped by a highly decorated frieze in a similar colour incorporating either pomegranate or acanthus leaf details, with cream tiling or paintwork above. The ticket offices featured highly stylised window surrounds made in most cases from faience, although a small number (mainly on the CCEHR) were of wooden construction. Flooring had a mosaic finish, mauve in colour. Lighting was provided by hexagonal shaded pendant fittings, while large round clocks (supplied by the Self Winding Clock Company of New York) were suspended from ornate brackets from the ceiling. At most stations, separate routes were provided for access to and egress from the lifts, which had wooden frontages on either side. The Otis electric lifts were supplemented by a spiral staircase, which was generally accessed by means of a straight flight with finishes matching those in the ticket hall.

However, in most cases the spiral staircase itself utilised the colour scheme prevalent throughout the lower levels of the station, with the tiles laid generally in a vertical stretcher bond to take account of the curvature of the shaft walls. The materials used were nine by three inch glazed earthenware tiles, supplied by

The booking hall at Gloucester Road, photographed in February 1928.

one of several firms including: G Woolliscroft & Son, Maws & Co (agents W B Simpson & Sons) and Craven Dunhill. In all but a few cases, this consisted of cream as the background with contrasting coloured bands as relief. The access passageways were generally fairly plain, making use of the colour scheme to be found on the platforms but in simplified form.

At platform level, individual bays were formed by tile bands extending over the soffit to the trackside wall. Each bay was occupied by one of three features – a panel of geometrical patterned tiling; a concrete portal leading to a passageway; or a plain panel containing the station name fired directly onto the tiling (three of which were to be found on almost every platform). The latter two were usually identified

through the use of double tile bands – a fact that can prove helpful in identifying the location of original features even if they have since been removed. Where the station name is located adjacent to an entrance or exit portal, it is possible to find four tile bands together, for example on the eastbound platform at Russell Square. The patterned panels differed considerably between stations, with few being identical. However, variations in format were necessary to reflect the varying width of individual bays. It is not the intention of this book to deal in detail with these tile patterns. A large, and undoubtedly definitive, book on these by Doug Rose is expected to be published within the next few years.

Further horizontal groups of coloured bands featured at waist level and across the top of the tiled sections. On many of the later stations (mainly on the CCEHR – e.g. Hampstead, Mornington Crescent), the lower panels (except below those containing the station name) were left as exposed render, possibly for use as

A Hampstead Tube platform at Euston at the time of opening in 1907. Note the station name within the tiling and the application of metal signs below.

advertising sites and/or as a cost saving measure. On most GNPBR stations (plus exceptional examples on the other two railways), signs were incorporated within the tiling itself, notably on the vertical tile bands at eye level, in cross-passageways at the base of staircases and on trackside walls within the horizontal band. Whilst there was some variation in execution between these 'WAY OUT' and 'NO EXIT' patches at different stations, these are perhaps the most distinctive and attractive features of Green's stations, at platform level at least.

Station layout

The layout of most stations followed a common theme. The ticket hall was located at street level, with two or more lift shafts and a spiral staircase leading down to the lower levels. From there separate entry and exit routes were provided, with staircases down to the platform tunnels. These were usually positioned at the same level, with the platforms themselves connected by means of cross-passageways. Obviously there were many exceptions to this standard format: for example, three stations had sub-surface ticket halls while a further three had each platform on a different level.

Whilst the simple nature of these stations aided their rapid construction, their layout left little scope for expansion to cope with traffic flows where greater than anticipated. The constraints imposed by the use of slow-moving lifts meant that many of the busier stations suffered from considerable congestion. The introduction of the escalator on the Underground (at Earl's Court in 1911) opened up new possibilities for the mass movement of passengers and around half of Green's stations had this new equipment installed in place of lifts, mainly during the 1920s and 1930s. In some cases, this resulted in the original ticket hall building being abandoned completely, for example at Dover Street (now Green Park) and Hyde Park Corner. In others, the buildings were retained as access points to new subterranean ticket halls, notably at Oxford Circus and Piccadilly Circus.

The price of success

For almost four years, Leslie Green's life revolved around the development of his generic design and overseeing its implementation on site. Despite the high degree of standardisation in terms of format and materials, each station building had its own problems to be identified and overcome – issues in which Green may have maintained a personal involvement.

There is some uncertainty as to the extent of Green's day-to-day input into the design of each station. Undoubtedly he headed the architectural team and developed the architectural philosophy adopted. However, much of the decision-making would have been left to the individual designer and, most pertinently, to those firms employed to undertake the work on site. This was particularly true of those responsible for the wall tiling and a close study reveals many similarities of décor between stations sharing a common building or tiling contractor. Nevertheless, the pressure of delivering so many stations to such tight timescales appeared to have an adverse effect upon Green's health and by early 1907 it was apparent that he was increasingly unable to continue with his workload as before. On 25 June of that year, George Gibb, the Managing Director of the UERL, wrote to him confirming that:

– his contract would be terminated so as to expire at the end of 1907;

– he would receive his salary up to the end of his contract;

– he would retain the title of Consulting Architect to the Underground Company without fee;

– he would receive £750 in consideration of the work he had done in connection with Underground tiling and any other work he had done not expressly included in his contract with the Company.

This last clause is of particular relevance as it indicates clearly that Green had a direct involvement in the specification and/or design of areas within the station and had not been restricted to the surface level buildings alone, as had been specified in his 1903 contract with the Company.

Decorative information at Russell Square, typical of Leslie Green stations.

A quiet day in the life of Russell Square station, after the canopy and vertical Underground sign had been added above the entrance.

Indeed, one could speculate that it was Green himself who suggested the inclusion of distinctive patterned panels within the wall tiling, given that one of the first BSWR platforms to have been completed, at Trafalgar Square (now Charing Cross), was clad with plain white tiling in the manner of the contemporary Central London Railway stations. Alternatively, it is possible that Yerkes himself conceived the new approach, based on his experience elsewhere, and that Green simply put the idea into practice.

Green's ill-health coincided with his becoming a Fellow of the RIBA and also the completion of almost all of his stations, the final line – the CCEHR – having opened in June 1907. That same month, he left England for recuperation, leaving supervision of the remaining works in the hands of his deputy, Stanley Heaps (who went on to succeed Green as Architect to the Underground Group). However, disease continued to plague him and despite a move to a sanatorium on the Norfolk coast, his health deteriorated further. Leslie Green died on 31 August 1908 at Mundesley-on-Sea from tuberculosis of the throat, leaving a widow Mildred (whom he had married in spring 1902) and a young daughter, Vera.

The stations today

The current condition of the many stations designed by Green varies quite considerably. There are some, such as Holloway Road and Tufnell Park, which have survived largely unchanged over the past 90 years plus. In contrast, there are others, Piccadilly Circus and Waterloo for instance, where next to nothing remains in public areas to remind us of his work. And of course, there are the majority where a significant proportion of the original fabric remains intact but has been substantially altered or has lost, say, the street buildings or platform tiling.

Furthermore, the day-to-day treatment of many of the stations, notably at platform level, has been less than sensitive. From the very early days, for example, commercial advertising was pasted extensively over the wall tiling, obliterating much of the patterning and even the signs. Whilst some control is now placed on such activities, the pressure for wall space means that often the architectural integrity of the finishes has had to be compromised.

The key purpose of this book has been to create a photographic record of Leslie Green's surviving work. Consequently, the primary focus has been on those stations where most of the original fabric survives, albeit disused or extensively restored in some cases. However the remaining 12 which have lost most, if not all, of their original features have not been ignored so that all buildings Green designed for London's tube railways are included.

A postscript

The world will never know what contribution Leslie Green may have made to architecture, or indeed possibly other fields, had he not died at just thirty-three years of age. In the years that followed up to and during the First World War, Stanley Heaps continued and evolved the style developed by Green for use on new stations on the Bakerloo Line extensions to Paddington and later Queen's Park. The buildings at Maida Vale and Kilburn Park in particular are often mistaken for works by Green, despite the fact he had died seven years before they were opened. It is to be hoped that Leslie Green's legacy will continue through the preservation of his surviving stations for as long as they persist in serving the purpose for which they were built.

Maida Vale station, opened in 1915 – designed by Stanley Heaps but following Green's general style. Note the absence of a frieze between the rectangular and arched windows, along with the shallow nature of the upper floor. The latter was made possible because no lift machinery was required, for the three stations on the Queen's Park extension of the Bakerloo Line were equipped with escalators from the start. Another station designed by Heaps in Leslie Green style is Kilburn Park.

ARSENAL

Operational stations with original features largely intact

THIS STATION, with the name 'Gillespie Road', opened on 15 December 1906 as part of the Great Northern, Piccadilly & Brompton Railway. Located just 690 metres to the south-west of the original terminus at Finsbury Park, it shares with that station the distinction of being the only bored tunnel tube station left on the Underground network whose platforms are accessible from street level via staircases only.

The name was changed to 'Arsenal (Highbury Hill)' on 31 October 1932 at the behest of the nearby football club of the same name, which at the time was rebuilding its Highbury stadium. The frontage of the ticket hall building (1) was renewed soon after in the austere architectural style of the period. The painted white façade looks somewhat out of keeping with its residential setting but is redeemed by a large mosaic roundel, which was renewed to its original 1932 specification in 1993.

The majority of the station's original features beyond the ticket hall remain intact including most of the wall tiling in the access passageways and platforms.

The ticket hall is located some distance away from the railway itself, requiring passengers to walk along lengthy sloping passageways to reach the staircases to the platforms. The initial length of passageway has a square cross-section, with a metal girder ceiling. The tiling to either side is in poor condition and much has had to be patch repaired or overpainted over the years. The passageway is split via a robust set of railings (replaced in 1998) which is used to segregate the heavy football traffic flows on match days from those passengers wishing to travel in the opposite direction – note the Underground roundel motif within the design. The two circular tunnels leading to the platforms bifurcate at this point (2) – an arrangement peculiar to this station.

1

The wooden clock (3) is a typical feature of stations of the Underground Group, and many have survived in good condition, including another one in Arsenal's ticket hall. The green tiled borders below once contained tiled directional signs but these have long been superseded by applied metal versions. The small white bay directly beneath the clock is a distinctive feature of tiling produced by Woolliscroft.

The mauve, white and green pattern seen in the view of the westbound platform (4) matches that found in the passageways. Although obscured by posters for many years, the original station name within the tiling has since been exposed and can be observed at several positions along the platform walls.

The help point system was installed in 1997 and particular attention was paid to the careful cutting out and replacement of individual tiles where conduits needed to be inserted into the render behind.

The remains of the original tiled sign 'TO HAMMERSMITH' may be observed beneath the 1993 vintage line diagram facing the westbound platform. Remnants of its counterpart on the eastbound platform ('TO FINSBURY PARK') are also visible.

Of the companies used to manufacture the tiles needed for Green's stations, those produced by G Woolliscroft & Son Ltd, along with those of Maws, have perhaps stood the test of time best. Certainly the platform tiling at Arsenal is still generally in fine condition, despite being over 90 years old. A tile bearing

the manufacturer's name is located in one of the cross-passageways at the western end of the platforms (5). Similar examples survive at Chalk Farm amongst other stations.

The station name was applied to the original frontage of the street-level building, as shown in the black and white photograph opposite, and to the tiling at platform level. Two of these former 'Gillespie Road' names have been preserved and restored to public view (6).

BELSIZE PARK

THE STATION opened on 22 June 1907 on the Hampstead branch of the Charing Cross, Euston & Hampstead Railway. The majority of the station's original features remain intact including the external façade and most of the wall tiling in the access passageways and platforms. The ticket hall, however, was modernised in the late 1980s in conjunction with lift replacement and UTS installation works.

The ticket hall building (1) has a standard faience façade, in this case with five symmetrical window bays separated by cartouche decoration (2). When opened, the station name was picked out in black lettering on a white background on the frieze directly beneath the cornice, but this had been removed by the 1960s. Similarly, 'HAMPSTEAD', 'TUBE' and 'RAILWAY' were once displayed above the second, third and fourth bays respectively, with 'UNDERGROUND' replacing the word 'Tube' circa 1908. Unlike many of Green's buildings, Belsize Park has not had additional floors constructed above, although there are plans to do so in the coming years subject to planning permission

being granted. Note the red vitreous enamel panelling around the entrance and exit bays, which was installed at the time of the ticket hall's modernisation.

The distinctive triangular pediment above the doorway to the left of the entrance is a common feature wherever access was afforded to the floors above. Similar examples survive at Edgware Road and Elephant & Castle. Original door fanlight features also remain in place at Aldwych and Tufnell Park but lack the triangular pediments.

Uniquely amongst Green's buildings still in use, Belsize Park is set back from the main building line, resulting in the creation of a small forecourt surrounded by Edwardian decorative railings and fronted by stone columns (3). Note the presence of bronzed poster frames dating from the late 1920s and retaining their swan-neck fittings, although unfortunately not the associated globe shades.

For over 80 years, the station had been served by the original wooden clad lifts. The introduction of more stringent safety legisla-

1

tion, allied with the requirement to install new ticketing equipment under the UTS project, resulted in the lifts being replaced and the ticket hall finishes upgraded. By 1990, the original cream tiling, with its green edging above and below, had been replaced by the modern design that exists today.

The only expanse of original ticket hall tiling to have survived is in the straight staircase leading down to the top of the emergency stairs (4). Note the green pomegranate frieze detail and the contrast with the red and cream tiling used throughout the lower areas of the station – the two finishes being separated by a standard pilaster feature.

Cream and red tiles were used on the platform walls of all three tube stations on the Hampstead branch, although the red is somewhat darker here (5) compared to that installed at its sister stations at Hampstead and Chalk Farm. This variation could stem from the fact that a different tile manufacturer was utilised at each of the three sites. In 1989, the repeated application of graffiti to the paintwork resulted in tiling being extended above name frieze level by 1.5 metres as a trial measure. This approach proved successful and was adopted at several other stations.

In 1990 a requirement to install power cables via the overbridges to the void under the platform led to the installation of vitreous enamel cladding, which unfortunately cuts across one of the original station names.

The face of the clock on the southbound platform has recently been restored, while the original ornate bracketry remains (6).

CALEDONIAN ROAD

THE STATION opened on 15 December 1906 as part of the Great Northern, Piccadilly & Brompton Railway. It is one of only two tube stations in use on the Underground network (Earl's Court being the other example) whose main lifts extend down directly from the ticket hall to platform level without the need for additional staircases.

The majority of the station's original features remain intact including the external façade and the wall tiling on the platforms. The ticket hall, however, was modernised in 1987 in conjunction with lift replacement and UTS installation works.

Whilst Caledonian Road has a superficially largely unchanged Green frontage (1), some subtle alterations have been made over the years. The lower mullions and transoms have been removed, giving the five semi-circular windows at first floor level a slightly awkward look. The original exit bay to the far right-hand side has been blocked in using metal panels, while the adjacent shop unit has been severely disfigured. The glazed canopy was added in 1994 and the left-hand side of the elevation renewed in fibre-glass several years earlier. Of more significance, however, is the raised, gilded lettering displaying the station name above the central bay: whilst this may appear to be original, archive photographs reveal that this feature was once located to the bay to immediately to its left (2). Despite these changes, the basic form has been retained and notable original features, such as the bay to the left of

the entrance and the raised 'EXIT' lettering, survive intact.

In common with Belsize Park and many other Leslie Green stations, the original ticket hall finishes were removed around 1987 in association with lift replacement and UTS installation works. One now needs to visit Holloway Road to visualise how they once looked. The replacement scheme is not unattractive but fails to relate to early features that do survive, such as the green tiling in the staircase leading down to the emergency escape route. The glazed

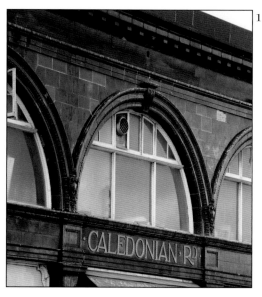

modernisation project. Note the trackside sign in the background.

Caledonian Road has a distinctive colour scheme, the two-tone mauve tiling without white or cream relief being unlike any other used on Green's stations (5). Furthermore, the station shares with Covent Garden (of finishes that survive) the feature of having a larger upper pattern than was usual on Green's designs. The tiling has survived in near perfect condition, with careful restoration carried out where required (6). Note the tiled name being displayed on a white background, unlike the cream used at most other stations. Furthermore, Caledonian Road is unique amongst stations whose finishes are still exposed in that the name is contained within a border, with the wording extending across two tiled bays. Note also the slight nick in the letter 'C' – a feature of tiled lettering on Woolliscroft stations.

The top section of the adjacent tiled sign was covered over for many years by a continuous name frieze, first added in the 1950s. When this was replaced in 1993, breaks were inserted deliberately in order to reveal the original sign's keystone feature. The name board (7) dates from around 1910 and is one of only four of this type which survive in situ on an operational station (two at this station and two at Covent Garden). It is a true ancestor of the modern London Underground roundel which is recognised around the world. Only at close distance can one determine that half of the nearby tiled name panel is in fact painted plaster, applied with great skill by a local artist during a refurbishment scheme in 1993.

Unlike at Arsenal, both the original tiled sign 'TO HAMMERSMITH' and 'TO FINSBURY PARK' survive in good condition, for the line diagrams which have obliterated so many other examples have been located further along each platform in the case of Caledonian Road. Note the highly stylised 'S' which contrasts with the plainer form of the other letters (8): compare this with a similar example, made by a different manufacturer, at Hyde Park Corner.

elevation to the rear belongs to the station control room, which was installed in 1996 as part of a multi-million pound project to provide improved passenger security equipment on the six Piccadilly Line stations around Finsbury Park.

The wooden fire hydrant cabinet at the top of the staircase (3) is an original feature which still serves the purpose for which it was intended.

The station was originally served by four lifts in two shafts. The second pair were removed from service prior to World War I and their shaft is now used for ventilation purposes. However, the unusual rendered portals which allowed access and egress are still visible (4), albeit now incorporated within the green and white tiling scheme used in the ticket hall during the 1980s

CAMDEN TOWN

THE STATION opened on 22 June 1907 forming the junction of the Hampstead and Highgate branches of the Charing Cross, Euston & Hampstead Railway. During the early planning stages of the line, the station was to have been called 'Camden Road' but its current name has been used throughout its time in passenger service. Its importance increased significantly in April 1924 when through services on the City & South London Railway (now the Bank branch of the Northern line) commenced.

Of the station's original features, only the Kentish Town Road façade and some wall tiling in the access passageways remain intact.

Unlike Chalk Farm and Leicester Square, Camden Town's two façades are not connected, with the apex being formed by a building in a completely different style and currently utilised as a bank. While the frontage facing Kentish Town Road remains largely as built, its counterpart on Camden High Street has undergone some significant changes over the years.

The black and white photograph (1) shows this elevation circa 1916: observe the spacing of the windows at first floor level and their relationship to the storey above. The station name lettering (which survived until the early 1960s) and ornate metalwork on top of the canopy are also worthy of note.

1

The photograph of the frontage today (2) shows some marked differences, which were brought about as a result of two major events affecting the station. Firstly in 1929, the three lifts which had served the station since it opened were replaced by two escalators leading down to a low level concourse, from which new passageways and staircases led to the platforms. This necessitated adjustments to the ticket hall, with the entrance, and its arched window directly above, being moved adjacent to the central bay. Secondly during the autumn of 1940, the left-hand third portion of the building was destroyed during an air-raid and has never been rebuilt.

The Kentish Town façade (3) includes several features of interest. Two of the early lamps suspended from ornate metal brackets survive, along with a bronze and blue vitreous enamel poster frame installed following the ticket hall alterations in the late 1920s, as was the Art Deco window to the right. The window to the left is contemporary with the opening of the station.

Access to and from the lifts was by means of a complex series of corridors and staircases at the southern end of the four platforms. Most of these routes were retained after the replacement of the lifts by escalators and have been used since as a means of interchange between the platforms.

The light blue and cream colour scheme used at Camden Town is in distinct contrast with those used on nearby stations, especially those on the Hampstead branch, but similar to that installed at Green Park. The tiling was until recently in poor condition, exuding an air of neglect at platform level. In order to address this, these finishes were replaced during spring 2001 in matching colour, although lacking the patterned bays and tiled names.

There is an interesting contrast at platform level between the original portals and those installed in the 1920s: whereas the former, with their distinctive keystone feature, are integrated within the wall pattern and are denoted by double tile bands on either side, the latter intrude, apparently at random.

Before the advent of metal line diagrams on trackside walls, the direction of travel was indicated by means of signs built within the horizontal tile band, directly opposite the access point onto the platform. One may be observed at the southern end of the northbound High Barnet branch platform and is the only example to have survived (in public view at least) on the stations built by the CCEHR. The destination shown (4) refers to the present-day Archway station.

CHALK FARM

DURING THE early planning stages of the line, the station was to have been called 'Adelaide Road' but its current name has been used throughout its time in passenger service. It opened on 22 June 1907 as part of the Hampstead branch of the Charing Cross, Euston & Hampstead Railway.

The majority of the station's original features remain intact including its two street elevations and most of the wall tiling in the ticket hall, access passageways and platforms.

Only two of the many station buildings designed by Green had elevations which converged at an acute angle, Leicester Square being the other example. Clad with the standard ox-blood faience, Chalk Farm boasts a total of

14 arched windows eight of which face onto Adelaide Road (1), making it the longest overall façade of stations on the Yerkes tube lines. Access to the ticket hall was possible originally from both sides but the Haverstock Hill entrance (2) was blocked off when a new ticket office was installed as part of the UTS programme. At ground floor level some original windows may still be observed but others have since been infilled, along with shop units which were once set into the façades (3).

As with Belsize Park, the station's name was originally displayed on the high level white frieze, with the name of the railway below the arched windows, but this wording had been removed by the early 1950s.

1

4

Tiled 'UNDERGROUND' signs were added above each entrance and the shop unit at the building's apex around 1908. The last of these (4) is uniquely on a curved section of frontage. Note the rectangular window with its distinctive pediment above – again an attribute shared with Leicester Square.

With very few exceptions, the detailing on the faience used by Green is quite subtle. Round windows (5) appear on many of his buildings but it is only when one studies them carefully that their intricate nature is revealed.

Unlike almost all other Green stations, most of Chalk Farm's original ticket hall finishes survived the UTS and lift replacement programmes (6). In this case, dark green tiling is used to frieze level, with a decorative course above. Note the wooden dado rails and lighter coloured green tile band at high level. The railings at the top of the stairs are contemporary with the station's opening and are similar in style to those found on the platforms at Golders Green. The wall tiling on the spiral staircase is a recent replacement in a similar style to the original but features a much darker red compared to that used elsewhere on the station.

The splendid clock (7) is an original feature of most, if not all, of Green stations and was utilised at both ticket hall and platform levels. Each one was manufactured by the Self Winding Clock Company of New York and cost just over £4 (a considerable amount of money at that time). All those that survive have since been converted to electricity.

The cream and red pattern here (8) is similar to those installed at its sister stations at Belsize Park and Hampstead. Originally the lower panels below each patterned bay were left as exposed render, possibly to allow for the application of pasted advertising in specific positions. Whilst this practice was followed for many years, it was eventually discontinued and the panels painted over. In 1993, the advent of graffiti vandalism led to the replacement of the render by red and cream tiling to match that used elsewhere. Other features of note are the presence of the station name on a white background, the unique deployment of ten courses of cream tiles between skirting plinth and the waistband (nine being the norm) and the remnants of tiled directional signs beneath trackside line diagrams. A fine example of a tile bearing the manufacturer's name is located near the base of the staircase leading onto the southbound platform.

COVENT GARDEN

THIS STATION was not complete at the time of opening of the Great Northern, Piccadilly & Brompton Railway and consequently was not brought into passenger service until four months later, on 11 April 1907.

The majority of the station's original features remain intact including the external façades and the tiling on the walls of the platforms and low level access areas. The ticket hall, however, was modernised around 1988 in conjunction with lift replacement and UTS installation works.

Covent Garden is one of the few Leslie Green buildings with two elevations at right-angles to each other (1). Both contain three arched windows, although they differ through the inclusion of small rectangular windows on the James Street façade. Unlike many sites, Covent Garden has retained its original ticket hall configuration, with passengers leaving the lifts pouring almost directly onto the street. The plain office block above was added around 1964, while the distinctive, glazed canopies were installed in 1993.

The small window at the junction of the two elevations is an unusual feature of this station,

as is the nature of the bas-relief lettering at first floor level. The use of dark grey text on a white background is more akin to the approach used on the CCEHR stations and is in distinct contrast to the gilding deployed elsewhere on the GNPBR. Only four other stations shared this characteristic. It should be noted that the lettering spelling out 'GARDEN' on the Long Acre frontage is not in fact original, for it replaced the word 'STATION' when the 'UNDERGROUND' patch was added within a year or so of the building opening.

The ticket hall was once clad with finishes typical of those used by Green in stations on the GNPBR. Dark green tiles in stretcher bond form clad the walls, with a moulded floral frieze at dado height. The walls above were painted but incorporated several fluted wooden bands as relief. The ticket office once featured beautiful, Art Nouveau window surrounds but only those at Holloway Road survive in their original condition. The appearance of the hall is now substantially different but the use of dark green wall tiling does present a visual link to the earlier design.

The wall tiling at Covent Garden has a most

1

distinctive pattern (2), making use of a deep orange tone similar to that installed at Tufnell Park. Several tiled directional signs have survived here and are still in operational use. Note the presence of arrows both above and below the text (3) compared with Russell Square which had a different tiling contractor.

An early wooden clock in its original case is located at the bottom of the staircase leading to the platforms (4). To the right of the line diagram, a tiny section of the original tiled directional sign may be detected. Parts of the versions on the trackside walls are also evident.

The tiling at Covent Garden (5) is in less than perfect condition, perhaps reflecting the station's heavy traffic flows over the years and the pressure for space for commercial use at this key central London location. Careful replacement of some areas of tiling, especially of the lower panels which are particularly prone to damage, was carried out in 1994. The 'Covent Garden' bar and disc name board (6) would have been added here and at other stations around 1910.

There is another example of a tile bearing the supplier's name, in this case located in a short corridor at the bottom of the spiral staircase (7).

EDGWARE ROAD

THE STATION opened on 15 June 1907 as the temporary terminus of the Baker Street & Waterloo Railway following its extension westwards from Great Central (now Marylebone). The original section of railway had opened on 10 March the previous year.

The vast majority of the station remained largely unchanged until extensive modernisation was carried out, in conjunction with UTS installation and a project to replace the wood panelled lifts. The latter necessitated closure of all facilities between 25 June 1990 and 26 January 1992. The main facade and some other small areas of interior tiling are the only original finishes to have survived this work.

Edgware Road possesses one of the simplest of frontages to a Leslie Green building (1). It contains the standard features but just two semi-circular windows; one above the entrance, the other above a shop unit. A unique feature of this BSWR station, however, is the reinstatement of individual lettering on the high level white frieze – a characteristic more commonly found on the CCEHR stations which also opened in 1907. Note the form of the capital G which looks like a C from a distance – a characteristic of this particular tiling contractor.

The black and white photograph (2) shows the station as it appeared in March 1933. Note the ornate metalwork on the canopy, the railway

name displayed on the frieze above the shop unit and the distinctive triangular pediment above the wooden door to the floor above (these last named are still evident today, albeit somewhat altered in appearance). The three storey buildings to the south of the station were demolished in the mid-1960s in order to allow the construction of the Westway flyover nearby.

The grille above the entrance (3) is not an early feature and was in fact installed during the late 1980s! However, it was based upon the much smaller lift and booking office ventilation grilles which still survive in the ticket hall (4,5). Of greater interest are the telephone signs on their ornate brackets to either side of the entrance, which probably date from no later than the 1920s.

Several Green stations, including Aldwych and Brompton Road, had two unconnected façades. However, Edgware Road was unique in having a secondary frontage (facing onto Bell Street) which was not faced in the standard ox-blood red faience tiling; brown glazed brickwork being used instead (6). The contrast in style calls into question whether Green, or indeed any architect, was involved in the design of this elevation, given the heavy pressure he was under to complete the main buildings of so many stations.

Until the 1980s, the central bay was used as the exit route from the lifts, with signs applied to the white panel above giving directions to use the main entrance on Edgware Road itself. The broad white band above this once proclaimed 'BAKERLOO RLY . EDGWARE ROAD' in large block letters, the fixing holes for which can still be observed. Note the early ornate lamp bracket.

A pair of pilasters facing each other near the entrance are the only original finishes to have survived in the ticket hall (7). However, as this

photograph shows, its overall appearance has been recreated almost exactly, along with some enhancements such as the chequered floor surface and signing to current standards. Particularly impressive are the replicated ticket office windows, hexagonal shade pendant light fittings and pomegranate tile bands at dado height. An early wooden clock is positioned on the wall at the far end of the ticket hall.

With the exception of some wall tiling in the spiral staircase and one station name, none of the original wall tiling was retained following the station modernisation project. Instead, a new scheme was adopted (8) which used the colours of the earlier design but in a simpler manner. Cream predominates, with brown used for borders and as a twin horizontal band throughout. All cables are contained within a bronzed trunking system, from which downlighting washes over the name frieze. Surviving elements include tile bands over the soffit, voussoirs around two of the tunnel mouths and

standard portals to all passageways and lift openings.

Like almost all station modernisation schemes carried out during the 1980s and 1990s, it was decided that the original tiling should not be removed prior to new finishes being applied. This presented the opportunity to retain one of the station names (at the southern end of the northbound platform), set back into the new tiling enclosed within a glazed brass frame (9).

ELEPHANT & CASTLE

FOLLOWING THE southward extension of the Baker Street & Waterloo Railway from Kennington Road (now Lambeth North), this station opened as the final terminus on 5 August 1906. The original section of line had opened on 10 March the same year. A nearby station of the same name serving the City & South London Railway had been operational since 18 December 1890.

The majority of the station's original features remain intact including the external façades and much of the tiling on the walls of the platforms and low level access areas. The ticket hall, however, was modernised in 1993 and paint now covers most of the platform walls.

In many ways, Elephant & Castle is a typical Leslie Green station – the ox-blood faience cladding, semi-circular windows at first floor level, tiled lettering and the like (1). Yet there are several features which make its surface building at least quite distinct. For example, the attractive three storey structure built above housed the South London Press organisation for many years and while now used by London Underground staff, it is still known as South London House. The red brick and stone used in its construction are typical of these over-station developments and similar examples may be observed at Leicester Square and Camden Town. The two façades are at an obtuse angle to each other, a characteristic shared with Gloucester Road and York Road of Green's surviving stations. Lettering, possibly metallic, proclaiming 'BAKER STREET AND WATERLOO RAILWAY' was once applied to the high level frieze below the cornice on the shorter of the two elevations, but no evidence of this feature now survives.

The door to the left of the entrance, with its associated pediment detail, is a good example of its kind (2). Others survive at Belsize Park and Edgware Road.

The closure of Skipton Street and the resultant creation of a small piazza presented an opportunity to create a more radical exit from the station than had previously been the case. In 1993, the breezeblock walls that had been used to fill in the bays at the time of UTS installation were removed and a glazed structure installed (3). It includes some of the very few automatic sliding doors on the Underground system.

Behind the extension may be observed the station name in gilded, raised lettering, although now largely obscured when viewed from ground level. Note the projecting sections of the cornice above the first and fourth bays, which line up with the stone windows of the South London House. This characteristic, which is repeated on the entrance frontage, was incorporated in a very small number of Green's stations, of which Elephant & Castle is the only one to have avoided demolition.

Almost none of the original ticket hall finishes survive, but the area once had the characteristic dark green wall tiling topped with a floral decorative band. Note the clerestory windows and skylights which allow natural daylight to enter. The modernised ticket hall includes a large mural panel displaying a scene of Elephant & Castle around 1912.

A simple, deep red and cream pattern is used for the tiling scheme throughout the lower levels of the BSWR station (4). However, extensive damage was carried out to the finishes on the platforms when preliminary investigations in association with a major modernisation project were commenced in May 1990. Unfortunately, the latter was suspended in September of the same year and little work has been undertaken since that time to rectify the situation. The platform tile pattern was unusual in that two subtly different shades of maroon were used, with a small contrasting motif positioned centrally within each bay. The tiling has since been patch repaired and painted over to improve the general ambience at platform level. Note the existence of two passageway portals directly adjacent to each other at the southern end – a unique characteristic of these platforms.

GLOUCESTER ROAD

Although the adjacent station on the Metropolitan Railway had been in service since 1868, the tube station opened on 15 December 1906 as part of the Great Northern, Piccadilly & Brompton Railway.

The majority of the station's original features remain intact including the external façades and wall tiling throughout the lower levels.

The exterior of this station (1) is almost unchanged since the GNPBR building was constructed during the Edwardian era. Extensive refurbishment of the short façades, each with just a single arched window, was completed in 1997: this included major work to overcome corrosion of the steel frame, along with the reinstatement of original features such as the metal bracketry for the lamps.

The bay facing onto Courtfield Road (2) once served as the exit from the GNPBR station. However, both entry and exit from the lifts has been via the main ticket hall concourse, shared with District and Circle Line users, since UTS installation in the 1980s. Note the semi-circular feature at the top of the pilaster and the poster panel inlaid into the faience. One of the original lift grilles may still be seen above an office window in the combined ticket hall.

Despite being in generally poor condition and largely covered with advertising and other furniture, the tiling on the platforms is arguably some of the most attractive installed on Green's stations. The patterning is fairly simple but it is the deep intensity of the dark green tiles which make their appearance so special. It is well preserved in the stairway shafts leading to and from the lifts (3). All the standard features are present – tiled signing, passageway entrances with their keystone feature, tiled trackside signs and voussoir decoration around the tunnel portals, plus sections of the original concrete

floor surface. A restoration scheme is planned for these areas and the potential for creating a much improved travelling environment is considerable.

The iron door at the eastern end of the eastbound platform (4) is an original feature, also found at several other Piccadilly Line stations, complete with a maker's plaque ascribing its manufacture to the St Pancras Ironworks Co. Note the moulding detail on two of the lower panels, similar to that found on contemporary windows.

GOLDERS GREEN

THE STATION opened on 22 June 1907 as the terminus of the Hampstead branch of the Charing Cross, Euston & Hampstead Railway.

Many of the station's original features remain intact including the ticket hall building (albeit partially obscured), wall tiling in the subways and staircases, and railings at platform level.

There is some doubt about the architect of this station. Whilst Leslie Green was responsible for the overall design of the ground level buildings on the three Yerkes tube railways, Golders Green bears little semblance to the other 37, externally at least. No red faience cladding and ornamental brackets, no semi-circular windows and tiled signing – the main station building is a simple brick structure, with three windows at first floor level facing in each direction.

When opened, a metal canopy proclaiming 'HAMPSTEAD TUBE' along its front was placed above the entrance but this was replaced by 1925 by a glazed canopy around the perimeter. Part of this was soon removed and a rather incongruous stone entrance block inserted in its stead. The 1980s saw the construction of a new ticket hall building in front of the original, albeit using similar materials.

At platform level, each staircase shaft is surrounded by metal railings dating from the station's construction (1) and which have similar counterparts at Chalk Farm and Belsize Park amongst others. The canopies, with their simple iron structural supports and wooden valances, are also original features.

The two main island platforms are accessed by means of separate way in and way out subways, each with dedicated staircases. Both subways and staircases are clad with wall tiling similar in style to that used at other Yerkes tube stations. An original grille may be found at the

base of one of the staircases leading from the northbound platform (2). Two sets of stairs pass by each other to give an unusual arrangement (3). Note the carved scrolled detail on the wooden handrail (4).

An early section of canopy to the left of the building facing the bus station has survived intact (5). Although the now disused secondary entrance post-dates Green's involvement at this station, it has two features that are worthy of attention. Opened on 18 December 1911 to provide interchange with the new electric tram routes along Finchley Road, this facility is accessed by means of a timber colonnade walkway. Above the entrance to the ticket hall itself is a delightful door pediment in white faience with raised lettering (6). It is unfortunate that this interesting architectural item is no longer available in public view.

GOODGE STREET

THE STATION opened, with the name 'Tottenham Court Road', on 22 June 1907 as part of the Charing Cross, Euston & Hampstead Railway. It was renamed 'Goodge Street' on 9 March 1908 in order to avoid confusion when interchange connection was made between the Central London Railway station at Tottenham Court Road and the CCEHR's Oxford Street.

Of the station's original features, only the ticket hall building and some isolated tiling in internal areas remain intact.

Goodge Street retains one of the less altered of Green's façades (1). All the red faience cladding is intact, as are the two original lamp fittings. Unlike many other stations, one bay is still in use for exiting traffic during the busiest times of the day. Black lettering proclaiming 'HAMPSTEAD RLY' was in place on the white band above this exit bay until around 1933. The elevation is unusual in that it has three rectan-

gular windows adjacent to each other, the outer two of which are above bays which were once small shop units but have since been blocked in with matching faience.

A unique feature of Goodge Street is the name frieze that extends the full width of the elevation at high level. When constructed, it featured the standard treatment used for most buildings on the CCEHR, that is black lettering on a white background stating the station's name. This was still in place until 1925, when the blue enamelled panel was installed. It is not known why this alteration took place, although it coincided with the building above being constructed and could have been an experimental measure to improve station identity.

When opened, the ticket hall was clad with typical CCEHR wall finishes – cream tiling with green friezes above and below. In the 1927 black and white photograph (2), note the wooden frontage to the lifts to the left and the

1

decorative grille above the standard tiled ticket office window to the right. Modernisation works in conjunction with lift replacement and UTS installation projects in the late 1980s led to the removal of all original features.

The finishes throughout the lower levels of the station were also replaced as part of the 1980s Station Modernisation Programme. However, some small areas survived, notably in the spiral staircase (3) and its access corridor at low level. As the photograph shows, light green was used as the relief colour in the tiling scheme: it is interesting to note the variation in tone that occurs as one descends the stairs – something that would not be accepted with today's manufacturing techniques.

The style of sash window frame sometimes found on the first floor of Leslie Green stations is to be found here in modern facsimiles on the ground floor detail (4).

HAMPSTEAD

THE STATION opened on 22 June 1907 as part of the Hampstead branch of the Charing Cross, Euston & Hampstead Railway.

Of the station's original features, only the ticket hall building and some isolated tiling in internal areas remain intact. Hampstead has one of Green's more unusual surface buildings, having two façades separated by a third splayed elevation (1). This is related primarily to the topography of the area, with both Heath Street and Haverstock Hill on considerable inclines. Several significant changes have been made to

added later above the main entrance. All of these were removed by the early 1960s. The bronzed poster frames date from the 1920s. Unusually there is a round window at low level (2).

Although very little of the original finishes in the ticket hall survive, a modernisation scheme completed in 1988 reinstated matching tiling and retained some early features (3). The ticket office windows and hardwood wooden doors have been reproduced accurately but the inclusion of acanthus leaf decoration within the frieze is incorrect, as the tiling originally lacked

the building over the years, notably the ugly metal structure on the roof above the Heath Street elevation which houses lift motor and ventilation equipment. Its addition also necessitated the installation of solid faience within the semi-circular windows on this side, which had been blocked in by 1955. The bay on the splayed elevation was originally the main entrance but this was blocked in during ticket hall modernisation works around 1988.

The names of the railway and station were once displayed on each elevation within the white bands at first and second floor level respectively. A tiled 'UNDERGROUND' sign was

this detail (a characteristic shared with Aldwych). The ceiling pattern, with its beams and covings, survives along with an early clock and its ornate bracketry.

The section of original tiling in the staircase leading from the emergency stairs (4) reinforces the assertion that acanthus leaf moulding was never included within the frieze at ticket hall level. Note the fine pilaster detail and the contrast with the maroon and cream tiling used throughout the rest of the station. The tiling on the platform walls that exists today was installed as recently as 1998 and is modelled on the colour and pattern used on the station when it

first opened, although the rendered panels found beneath most of the tiled bays were not retained. The original finishes were provided by the Permanent Decorative Glass Company and like those at other stations by the same firm (e.g. Tufnell Park and Mornington Crescent), did not survive decades of wear in good condition, resulting in their eventual replacement. One panel was retained, largely because it features the station name 'Heath Street' used throughout the planning stages of the railway. Unlike Warren Street and Arsenal, which also have examples of earlier names, the station opened as 'Hampstead', indicating that the change of title occurred shortly before, leaving insufficient time to amend the tile detail (5).

HOLLOWAY ROAD

THE STATION opened on 15 December 1906 as part of the Great Northern, Piccadilly & Brompton Railway. The majority of the station's original features remain intact including the external façade and internal finishes throughout.

Missing its cornice and having had its exit bay bricked in, this once splendid elevation is in poor condition, despite retaining its full complement of gilded raised lettering (1). An unusual feature is the presence of six adjacent arched windows at first floor level, with no rectangular windows in between. The canopy above the entrance was installed by the mid-1920s and replaced the tiled 'UNDERGROUND' signed applied around 1908. The bronze poster frames beneath were added in the 1920s and retain their swan-neck fittings. The bay adjacent to the shop unit contains a distinctive inset panel, once used for the display of large system maps printed on to vitreous enamel panels.

A distinctive feature of Holloway Road is the inclusion of the initial letters of the name of the railway, as well as the title of the station itself, on the façade. The bay below forms the entrance to an access road and features iron gates dating from the station's opening in 1906. Note also the cartouches at each end.

The ticket hall (2) is unquestionably the most complete of any on Green's surviving stations in public view. Of particular interest are the three tiled ticket office windows, which are the only original examples to have survived in an operational station (although reproduction versions have been installed at Edgware Road). Their sills were once tiled but severe cracking led to their replacement using bronzework during UTS modification works. Above, the original ceiling cornices remain, with complementary lighting installed in 1993, albeit to a contemporary design.

The fire hydrant cabinet (3) is original and is amongst the last to have survived at ticket hall level, although it was once located somewhat awkwardly against the central column. The wooden panelling behind probably dates from the 1920s but the wooden battens within the plasterwork, the frieze with a pomegranate design and the poster border within the tiling by the entrance are all contemporary with the station's opening.

The wooden clock, iron railings and fluted post supporting the handrail are original features still fulfilling the purpose for which they were intended (4), as is the original door by the ticket office (5).

The wall tiling throughout the lower levels of the station (although absent in the spiral staircase) features the standard cream background with bold, two-tone brown bands as relief. In the access corridor the portals to two shafts can be seen (6) – one occupied currently by two lifts, the other once containing the spiral moving walkway for which this station is well known.

The corridor and staircases leading from the rear of the lifts are now disused, although their access points may be observed from one of the platform cross-passageways and at the base of the spiral staircase. The original exit route from the platforms is now used for traffic in both directions.

The spiral moving walkway was the brainchild of the American engineer Jesse Reno, one of the key players in the development of escalators during the 1890s. While living in London, he developed the walkway concept and managed to arrange for one example to be installed at Holloway Road on the GNPBR. It consisted of a double helix, with a continuous platform moving at 100 feet per minute in each direction. Some confusion exists as to whether the equipment was ever brought into passenger service (albeit for a single day) or was in fact deemed unsafe from the beginning. Either way, it was largely dismantled in 1911 and now only the shaft remains. However, some of the lower sections of the machine were discovered during engineering works around 1992 and these are now held by London's Transport Museum at its depot in Acton.

The platforms remain in good condition (7), having been restored in 1993 shortly before the installation of help points and other security measures. Most of the tiled station names have survived, along with directional signs on the trackside walls and in the cross-passageway which once served as the entrance point onto the platforms.

One of the original cross-passageways has been closed off for many years and now contains an electrical switchroom.

HYDE PARK CORNER

THE STATION opened on 15 December 1906 as part of the Great Northern, Piccadilly & Brompton Railway. A new ticket hall and escalators were brought into service on 23 May 1932, with further modifications to the access routes in the early 1960s in association with the construction of the nearby road underpass.

Many of the station's original features remain intact including the external façade and finishes on the platforms.

It is unlikely that many of the patrons of the Pizza on the Park restaurant realise that they are sitting in what was once the ticket hall of an Underground station! Yet for over a quarter of a century, this building (1) was the entrance to Hyde Park Corner station and despite the removal of mullions from the arched windows and station name lettering, it is still clearly identifiable as one of Green's works. The left and right hand bays once served as the entrance and exit respectively, although none of the original internal finishes survive in public view.

Until recently, the platform level finishes were in particularly poor condition, having been largely untouched for many years. A £5 million enhancement project was completed in 2000

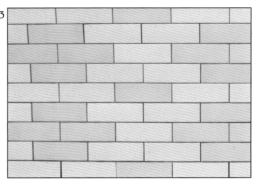

and resulted in all wall tiling being carefully restored, missing sections of tiles reinstated and new flooring installed (2,3,4). This scheme illustrates how investment can create an environment that is attractive and functional whilst retaining and enhancing the best of the original features. Note the introduction of a prototype cable management cum illumination system in place of the fluorescent strip lighting that existed previously. Breaks in the name frieze have been inserted in order to expose the full height of 'WAY OUT' and 'NO EXIT' artwork within the tiling. Compare the green surrounds to these features with those found elsewhere on the Piccadilly Line, such as at Gloucester Road.

Hyde Park Corner is one of only two stations (Holloway Road being the other) to retain the original directional signs at platform level (5). The examples illustrated are located in the cross-passageway which once served as the entrance route onto the platforms before the installation of escalators moved the access point to their eastern end. On the westbound platform, the overbridges leading to and from the lifts may still be observed.

The tiled direction signs 'To Hammersmith' and 'To Finsbury Park' facing the platforms are rare surviving examples of features that once existed at all the GNPBR tube stations. The introduction of escalators meant that the metal line diagrams, introduced as their replacements in the 1930s, were provided in a different location, resulting in them being overlaid with advertising posters but not destroyed. The enhancement project restored these splendid features to general view once again.

KENTISH TOWN

THE STATION opened on 22 June 1907 as part of the Highgate branch of the Charing Cross, Euston & Hampstead Railway. Escalators replacing the original lifts were brought into service in November 1932, while the ticket hall was remodelled again in 1980 to serve both Underground and national rail services.

Of the station's original features, the ticket hall building and much of the tiling throughout the deep level areas remain intact. Kentish Town's wide façade has its arched windows in a two-one-two arrangement and retains the original raised lettering at high level – one of only three examples to have survived (1). However the Hampstead Railway wording was removed at the time of escalator installation.

The canopy was first installed above the far left-hand bay when this served as the entrance. It was resited to the adjacent bay in conjunction with works which changed the layout of the ticket hall. Unfortunately, much of the ground floor is now in poor condition, having been crudely infilled or occupied by garish shop frontages.

Most of the access passageways and staircases leading to the platforms are clad with tiling in the original colour scheme. Also to be seen are the portals which once afforded access to and from the lifts (2).

In common with other stations opened in 1907, the pattern within the platform wall tiling is relatively simple and lacking in colour contrast, certainly in comparison with many of those on stations opened the previous year. Nevertheless, the finishes at Kentish Town are quite attractive where still exposed. The station names are currently obscured from view having been painted over (3).

An example of an original clock, recently refurbished with its ornate bracket, survives on each platform (4).

2

3

4

LAMBETH NORTH

WHEN THE STATION opened, on 10 March 1906 as the temporary terminus of the Baker Street & Waterloo Railway, it carried the name 'Kennington Road'. The line extended southwards to Elephant & Castle on 5 August of the same year, coinciding with the station being renamed 'Westminster Bridge Road'. Its name was changed again to 'Lambeth (North)' on 15 April 1917 and finally to its current form around 1928.

Few of the station's original features remain intact: those that do include the external façade and tiling on the walls of some access areas. The ticket hall was modernised around 1988 and the platforms in 1993.

As recently as 1990, the façade on Westminster Bridge Road (1) was covered with cream paint. Thankfully, this has since been removed to reveal the standard faience cladding beneath.

The ticket hall originally occupied the right-hand portion of the building and the arrangement was altered around 1930 when conversion for use as a staff training school took place. Some evidence of the training school's former role as the station ticket hall may still be observed in the entrance lobby, despite its not having served in this capacity for over 70 years. The decorative frieze and moulded advertising panel surrounds are clearly identifiable beneath the white paint, while the mauve mosaic floor is fully exposed – an extremely rare survivor.

Although the finishes and fittings are not original, the ticket hall has retained the feel of an Edwardian station through the use of green wall tiling (with simplified frieze detail) and pendant light fittings (2). A plaque, commemorating the factory owned by the Maudslay family on whose land the station was built, has been added to a wall near the ticket office and is of considerable interest.

The iron railings at the top of the emergency staircase route (3) are contemporary with the station's opening, as is the area of mosaic flooring behind.

Only a small section of the original tiling which once lined all the walls at street level survives, in the basement passageway at the top of the emergency staircase. The acanthus leaf motif on the rich green tiling contrasts with the dark blue, cream and gold staircase finishes in the background (4).

Much of the tiling in the subways leading from the lifts has been replaced in a matching style, with the cream extended over the soffit as a graffiti-prevention measure (5). The cream flooring was installed at the same time. Lambeth North was the only BSWR station to have directional signs incorporated within the tiling but unfortunately these were destroyed when replacement work took place.

The walls at platform level were in dire condition following three quarters of a century of wear and tear. The contrast with the environment that exists today (6) could not be more striking! The wall and soffit finishes have been replaced to a near identical pattern, with additional elements – floor tiling, signing to current standards, modern seating – adding to the general ambience, although it is unfortunate that neither the 'Way Out'/'No Exit' artwork (the only such feature to appear within the finishes of a BSWR station) nor the 'Kennington Road' panels were recreated. Both Lambeth North and Elephant & Castle are lacking the standard voussoired tunnel portals found originally at almost all other Green stations.

LEICESTER SQUARE

THE STATION opened on 15 December 1906 as part of the Great Northern, Piccadilly & Brompton Railway, with platforms for the Charing Cross, Euston & Hampstead Railway coming into service on 22 June the following year. Between October 1930 and May 1935 much of the station was reconstructed, with the provision of a new sub-surface ticket hall, escalators in place of the lifts and new entrances to street level. An additional subway route between the two sets of platforms was opened in July 1948. Only the street building of the station's original features remains intact and in public view.

At first glance, Leicester Square station's street level structure (1) resembles closely its contemporary at Chalk Farm, for both have two façades at an acute angle occupying the junction of two roads (in this case, Charing Cross Road and Cranbourn Street). However, closer inspection reveals some significant differences. For example, Leicester Square lacks the bay feature between the two elevations and any evidence of two tiled 'UNDERGROUND' signs which once existed.

On the other hand, both stations share a distinctive characteristic not to be found on any other Green building – a suite of three adjoining rectangular windows with a connecting pediment above, known collectively as a Palladian window (2). This is to be found at each end of both façades at Leicester Square and on the apex at Chalk Farm. Of interest is the scroll detail at the top of the intermediate columns between each window (3).

Another unique feature is to be found at the eastern end of the Cranbourn Street frontage. A sign in raised lettering within the faience indicates that the building above once housed the offices of the company which produced the famous cricketing almanac and other sporting equipment (4).

MARYLEBONE

THE STATION opened, with the name 'Great Central', on 27 March 1907 as the temporary terminus of the Baker Street & Waterloo Railway following its extension westwards from Baker Street. It was located close to the Marylebone terminus of the Great Central Railway which had opened just eight years before. The tube line extended further to Edgware Road on 15 June the same year. The current station title was adopted on 15 April 1917. In early 1943, the lifts were replaced by escalators accessed from the concourse of the adjacent Marylebone main line station.

The original station building was destroyed by bombing during World War II, while much of the platform tiling was replaced as part of an extensive enhancement project completed in 1990. Nevertheless, many original finishes survive in the low level access areas.

The street level building at Marylebone was rather different in appearance to the vast majority of structures designed by Green for the Underground Group. It consisted of a single storey, which may be explained by the ticket hall being at basement level and therefore a second floor not being required for the lift machinery. As a result, the building lacked the characteristic arched windows (1). In other respects, however, it was typical of Green's other work, through use of red faience and tiled lettering, for example. It once stood on the northern side of the junction of Harewood Avenue and Harewood Road – the site currently being occupied by the Jarvis Hotel. A subway link

between the building and the Great Central Railway terminus concourse was provided, which could explain why the ticket hall had been located at basement level.

The layout of the station altered substantially following the introduction of escalators. The lift shafts remained in place but a wide corridor was constructed to afford access to the new facilities.

The low level passageways and staircases retain their 1907 vintage cream and green-trimmed wall tiling: this has since been extended over the soffits and floor tiling installed in place of asphalt (2). The doorway to the right in this view leads to the emergency spiral staircase, no longer in public use.

As at Lambeth North (qv), the wall tiling at platform level was in poor condition by the late 1980s. Prior to the enhancement project commencing, restoration was the preferred course of action. However, initial attempts to remove the render panels beneath each tiled bay without damaging adjacent tiling proved futile and so a decision was made to undertake comprehensive replacement instead. The original pattern was reproduced (albeit set out slightly too high) and tiled borders were created to house advertising posters. New trunking, signing and floor tiling were also installed (3).

Both platforms, and indeed all those served by the BSWR, were extended by around 26 metres in the late 1930s to accommodate seven

car trains. These later sections were characterised by the absence of tile patterns, a slight 'set back' in the wall and the loss of the original keystone feature at the tunnel mouth (4).

Despite the renewal of almost all the wall tiling, one original panel has been retained, for it displays the name of the station at the time of opening. This piece of active conservation is to be applauded (5).

MORNINGTON CRESCENT

THE STATION opened on 22 June 1907 as part of the Charing Cross, Euston & Hampstead Railway. It was closed on 23 October 1992 in order to undertake modernisation and lift replacement works, but budgetary constraints meant that it was not reopened for six years.

The street level building has been beautifully restored (1). All the standard features are present – station name made up of individual tiled letters, cantilevered lamp brackets, bronze poster frames. The wooden windows and doors are a combination of originals and replicas. Given the apparent authenticity of its appearance, it is interesting to note that when the station opened, access was gained by means of an extremely narrow doorway on the left-hand side of the smaller of the two elevations. It was only much later that the existing entrance was opened up in place of a shop unit which previously occupied the site. On the elevation facing on to Hampstead Road the word STATION is incorrectly spaced owing to the two letter T tiles being transposed.

Wooden panels screen the emergency escape route from the station and are similar to those that once clad the exits from the lifts but are in fact reproductions (2). The grilles however are original fittings.

The ticket hall looks for all intents and purposes as if it retains its original finishes and fixtures, when in reality almost everything is reproduction (3). Nevertheless, the image is most attractive and illustrates what a Green station may have looked like in its heyday. Note the wooden ticket office windows. In common with most stations on the CCEHR, the lower sections of wall are clad with green coloured tiling.

The staircase balustrade (4) is one of the very few original fittings to have survived. Note the detailing around the top of the metal pillars, along with the wooden fire hydrant cabinet and reproduction wall tiling.

The desperately poor condition of the platform wall tiling meant that restoration was not a serious option, resulting in full replacement being chosen as the preferred cause of

1

action (5). While the same colours were used, the tiling scheme failed to include any significant areas of pattern, thereby adopting a similar approach to Edgware Road completed several years previously. Unlike Edgware Road, however, in this case the station name has not been encapsulated but recreated on the new tiling. The two stations also share the use of back-wall illumination, which creates a most attractive lighting effect. Note the retention of an original bracket to which a modern sign has been fixed (6).

OXFORD CIRCUS

THE STATION OPENED on 5 August 1906 on the original section of the Baker Street & Waterloo Railway, with an interchange link being provided to separate facilities serving the Central London Railway which had opened six years earlier.

The BSWR ticket hall was resited to basement level during 1912–14, concluding with the installation of escalators in place of lifts. This ticket hall was subsequently enlarged to serve both lines, with escalators to the Central London's platforms brought into service in June 1925.

The construction of the Victoria line, which opened at this station in March 1969, led to the provision of a completely new circular ticket hall beneath the junction of Oxford Street and Regent Street. The earlier facility beneath Argyle Street remains in service, however, and is used for exit traffic only.

Only the street building of the station's original features remains intact in public view.

Oxford Circus is interesting in that it offers a opportunity to compare and contrast the BSWR building with its slightly older CLR counterpart on the opposite side of Argyle Street. Both are two storey structures with lift machinery on the upper floor and each clad with faience – BSWR in red terra cotta, the CLR brown and unglazed.

Gilded metallic lettering proclaiming BAKER STREET AND WATERLOO RAILWAY was once displayed just below the cornice on each elevation, while the station name is still to be seen using raised letters on the faience itself. Prior to the layout modifications, the entrance to the ticket hall was via the right-hand bay on the Oxford Street frontage, with exit from the left-hand bay in Argyle Street (1). As will be seen from the photograph, commercial signs now clutter the ground floor.

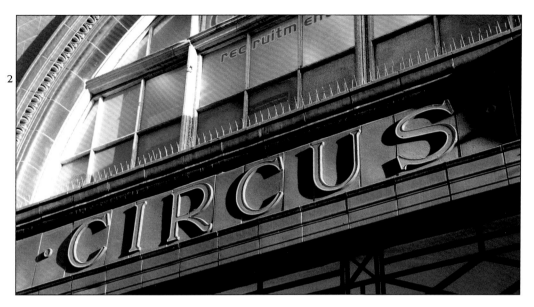

The lettering on the Oxford Street frontage (2) may appear to have remained largely unchanged since 1906 but this is in fact untrue, for it has an interesting story to tell. When the station building opened, the wording was 'OXFORD' and 'CIRCUS' beneath the two arched windows, with 'STATION' above the small doorway in between. Within two years, the lettering above the right-hand bay had been replaced by the tiled 'UNDERGROUND' sign being installed at most Yerkes tube stations to engender a sense of corporate identity. During the 1920s, this had in turn been obliterated following the installation of a metal canopy. The latter's eventual removal revealed the earlier signing, albeit in poor condition. Finally, in 1994, the original style of lettering was re-instated.

As noted above, this lettering is not original but has been created in a matching style to denote the doorway which gives the access to London Underground's offices in the building above. The detailing within the arch is worthy of particular attention (3).

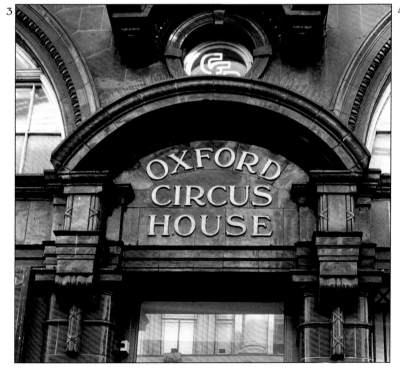

Examples of this monogram on the corner (4), depicting **U**nderground **E**lectric **R**ailways, were once to be found on several of Green's buildings but this is the only one to have remained intact.

REGENT'S PARK

OPENED ON 10 March 1906 on the original section of the Baker Street & Waterloo Railway, the majority of Regent's Park station's features dating from that time remain intact, including tiling in the entrance subways and wall finishes throughout the lower areas.

Regent's Park is one of the few Yerkes tube stations which has never had a prominent street presence. Indeed, access has always been by means of stairs off the pavement on the southern side of Marylebone Road, although when opened, these were set back some five metres or so from the kerbside (1).

The wrought iron railings feature a 'squashed' circle motif which is similar to those found at the top of staircases at Aldwych and Brompton Road stations. These appear to have once formed the original garden fence, which may be observed in the background of the photograph from around 1909 (2). Two splendidly ornate signs were in place – one at the top of each staircase – until the early 1930s. The railings in the foreground were removed in the early 1970s when carriageway alterations resulted in the current pavement arrangement.

Although the walls to the staircases themselves have been reclad in recent years, the rendered entrances to the subways leading to the ticket hall survive (3). Note the keystone feature (similar to those found on the platform portals) and decorative grille above each passageway mouth.

The walls of the subways retain some of the best examples of wall tiling from the early Tube

1

2

BAKER STREET & WATERLOO
ELECTRIC RAILWAY
STATIONS.

EDGWARE ROAD.   PICCADILLY CIRCUS.
GREAT CENTRAL.   TRAFALGAR SQUARE.
BAKER STREET.   CHARING CROSS
REGENT'S PARK.   WATERLOO.
OXFORD CIRCUS.   WESTMINSTER BRIDGE Rᴅ.
                    ELEPHANT & CASTLE.

BAKER STREET & WATERLOO
RAILWAY
REGENTS PARK STATION

EXIT

BAKERLOO TUBE

stations (4). The deep green finish, with its acanthus leaf frieze, creates a most atmospheric entrance to the station. The tiling on the soffits was applied in 1992 in order to address graffiti and water ingress concerns and this, along with the concrete paved floor, have enhanced the environment still further.

In contrast to the entrance subways, the ticket hall has been extensively modernised, the work being completed in 1986 in conjunction with UTS installation (5). Nevertheless there are several features of interest, such as the reproduction hardwood panels adjacent to the lifts, light fittings with hexagonal shades suspended from deep, riveted beams and an early fire hydrant cabinet. A small section of original wall tiling survives at the top of the emergency staircase.

The two 'Arts and Crafts' iron grilles, positioned at high level above the two lifts (6), are rare examples of their type to remain in situ along with those at Mornington Crescent and Edgware Road.

Particular reference should be made to the unusual layout of the emergency staircase, which unlike almost all other Green stations occupies only half of the available space in the circular shaft, the remainder being used for ventilation purposes and occupied previously by a third lift (7).

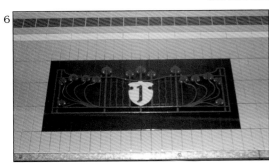

The finishes in the lower levels of the station retain their original colour scheme, although the tiling around the lift entrances and within certain panels on the platforms has in fact been replaced to match in more recent years. Note the portals to the lift shaft (8).

The platforms were the subject of an 'enhanced renovation' project, completed in 1991, resulting in the tiling being restored, extended and in small areas replaced to match, new flooring installed and a cable trunking provided at high level (9). However, the restoration work was not undertaken to the same standard as some later refurbishment schemes and the fixing holes for old roundels and other platform items may still be observed. A fine example of a tile bearing the manufacturer's name (in this case, W B Simpson & Sons) is located adjacent to the exit portal leading from the southbound platform.

RUSSELL SQUARE

THE STATION opened on 15 December 1906 as part of the Great Northern, Piccadilly & Brompton Railway. All of the station's original features remain intact with the exception of the ticket hall, which was modernised in the late 1980s in conjunction with lift replacement and UTS installation works.

Russell Square is arguably the most attractive of all Leslie Green's surviving stations (1). A major refurbishment scheme completed in 1995 resulted in restoration of the red faience and the reinstatement of lamp brackets (2) and the tiled signing. Unlike many of its contemporaries in central London, this station was never built over and it is interesting to note the matching sections of terrace on either side, showing how the railway intruded into this district of late Georgian London.

The tiled 'UNDERGROUND' sign (3) was added to the frontage around 1908, as it was at most other stations, following the decision made at the London Passenger Traffic Conference the previous year to co-ordinate the identity of all the tube railways using a common symbol. This feature was obscured beneath an ugly metal canopy installed in the 1920s until the latter's removal during the refurbishment project. The bronzed lamp brackets and their hexagonal shades are in fact replicas, modelled on similar examples found at Gloucester Road.

4

The 1906 ticket hall finishes remained largely intact until modernised in the late 1980s. A taste of how this area once looked may be gained from a surviving section of green tiling, to be found in the staircase leading to emergency stairs (4). In this example, no floral embellishment is included at dado height. A congestion relief scheme completed in 2002 replaced the existing white wall finishes with tiling which uses that present in the lower areas of the station as its theme.

Along with Covent Garden, Russell Square is the only GNPBR station in passenger service which retains signs in the passageways and staircases directing passengers towards the platforms or the lifts. There are nine examples at this site, of which two are illustrated (5,6).

Note too the original wall tiling and the cream mosaic added to the tunnel ceilings as an anti-graffiti measure.

The platforms were extensively refurbished in the mid-1990s and this included restoration of the wall tiling, with its distinctive chevron patterns, re-signing and the replacement of the asphalt floor surface by more attractive, green paving (7). All six of the tiled names survive (8), although two have individual letters obscured by injudiciously positioned switchrooms. The horizontal trackside tile band was moved up by several metres in order to allow the unimpeded posting of advertisements. Note the existence of a very unusual quadruple set of tile bands adjacent to the exit from the eastbound platform.

5

6

7

8

BUILT ADJACENT to the Metropolitan Railway's 1868 terminus of the same name, the tube station was not complete at the time of opening of the Great Northern, Piccadilly & Brompton Railway. Consequently it was not brought into passenger service until 24 days later, on 8 January 1907.

During 1973/74 escalators were installed between the deep level platforms and a new combined ticket hall in the former Metropolitan part of the station, replacing the lifts and separate ticket hall within the Green building. Although no longer in passenger use, Green's 1907 façade (1,2) remains largely as constructed, directly to the right of the white terracotta entrance to the arcade designed by George Sherrin which still serves as access to the station.

With Gloucester Road, South Kensington shared the distinctive feature of one-storey extensions, in this case on both sides of the main frontage. The one to the left once housed

2

3

entrance and exit routes into the ticket hall, while its counterpart (since demolished) provided an exit facility only. While most mullions and transoms have been removed from the arched windows, reflecting their revised role in tunnel ventilation, the frontage does retain within the faience a full complement of recessed bays which were used previously for publicity material.

Of particular note is the presence of raised black lettering displaying the station's name on the lower of the two white friezes (3). This appears to be an original feature and is thus a unique example of its kind. The letterform is interesting for it is not of standard block form, as illustrated by the presence of several serifs. Other lettering denoting the respective entrance and exit points has been removed however, presumably at the time of the construction of the joint ticket hall. Although the platforms were extensively modernised around 1988, several original features may still be observed, notably the tile bands over the soffits and the keystone portals around each entrance and exit (4).

The two platforms were constructed at different levels in order to afford level interchange with a proposed (but unbuilt) express line operated by the District Railway. This necessitated the lifts from the ticket hall stopping twice – at depths of 60ft and 78ft – to serve the eastbound and westbound platforms respectively. Some of the access points to the lift shafts may still be observed at platform level.

4

TUFNELL PARK

THE STATION opened on 22 June 1907 as part of the Highgate branch of the Charing Cross, Euston & Hampstead Railway. The ticket hall was remodelled around 1987 to allow for the installation of UTS equipment. All of the station's other original features remain intact .

Tufnell Park is in many ways a fine example of a Leslie Green building, occupying the corner site at the junction of Tufnell Park Road and Brecknock Road (1). Much of the faience remains in good condition, although some sections have been replaced over the years, while four original lamp brackets remain in position. However, the bays beneath each of the arched windows have been altered substantially, with three having been filled in with matching faience blocks. The left-hand bay on the Brecknock Road elevation was previously a shop frontage but now forms part of the entrance into the ticket hall.

The black and white photograph (2) shows the exterior of the station as it looked in 1925. Note the black lettering on the white friezes and

1

the vertical, block sign – an early form of corporate identity. Of particular interest is the tiled 'UNDERGROUND' sign which, unlike those at all other stations where it was installed around 1908, has been fitted at high level, just below the cornice. This feature had been removed by the mid-1950s.

Note the fine detailing around the original fanlight and door frame located to the right-hand side of the Brecknock Road elevation (3).

Although much altered over the years, most notably during the 1980s, the ticket hall has many original features (4). The ticket office was once contained behind the angled wall to the rear – an unusual arrangement which meant that passengers had to pass by the lifts if they needed a ticket. This layout proved unacceptable with the introduction of modern ticketing systems and the office was consequently moved nearer to the entrance. An original clock is suspended from an ornate metal bracket attached to the ceiling beam.

The ticket hall includes several early features including the metal balustrade and wall tiling to the emergency staircase (5), although the wooden ticket office window is in fact a 1980s version. Likewise, the large Art Nouveau iron grilles over the entrance are copies of the one installed at Edgware Road, which is itself a later feature influenced by the smaller lift ventilation grilles still surviving at some Leslie Green stations e.g. Regent's Park.

The tiling throughout the lower levels of the station has an orange and cream colour scheme not dissimilar to that at Covent Garden. Much of it is now in poor condition, although most of the tiled names are still exposed (6).

Both the ornate bracketry to the sign and the clock behind are early features worthy of preservation. The portal to the passageway is a standard feature of Green's Underground stations (7).

WARREN STREET

THE STATION opened, with the name 'Euston Road', on 22 June 1907 as part of the Charing Cross, Euston & Hampstead Railway. It was renamed 'Warren Street' on 7 June 1908 in order to avoid confusion with the similarly named 'Euston' station on the CCEHR. Escalators were installed in place of lifts, along with the construction of a new ticket hall, during 1933/34.

Of the station's original features, only the wall tiling in some passageways remains following its recent replacement at platform level.

Prior to its reconstruction in the early 1930s, Warren Street was extremely unusual in that whilst several other stations had separate elevations (e.g. Aldwych, Brompton Road), its two almost identical façades were back-to-back rather than at right-angles to each other – one facing Euston Road (1), the other Warren Street (2). Following the renaming of the station in 1908, alterations were made to the façades (3). Note the introduction of the 'UNDERGROUND' sign, the large system map and the use of 'RLY' instead of 'TUBE'.

The access subway leading to the south-bound Northern line platform retains its original finishes, in this case cream tiling with a dark blue border (4). Additional tiling has been applied over the soffits in order to minimise the impact of graffiti attack and to reduce maintenance costs. Furthermore, these finishes have been extended to cover those installed in the 1930s when links were made to the newly installed escalators.

Until late 2000, the 1907 vintage wall tiling had remained largely intact despite the ravages of the previous 90 plus years. However, much of it was in poor condition and this led to the decision being taken to undertake replacement of the finishes in matching style (5).

However unlike the comparable scheme at Lambeth North, some of the 'WAY OUT' and 'NO ENTRY' patches have been recreated, albeit at a lower level to avoid conflict with the name frieze. The overall effect is most pleasing and shows what can be achieved with sufficient attention to detail. One of the tiled signs with the original name (6) has been retained.

3

4

ALDWYCH

The station opened, with the name 'Strand', on 30 November 1907 as part of the Great Northern Piccadilly & Brompton Railway. It was originally planned that the station would form the southern terminus of the Great Northern & Strand Railway but when the GNSR merged with the Brompton & Piccadilly Circus Railway in 1901, the Holborn to Aldwych section was left as a spur of the main line. In order to avoid confusion with 'Charing Cross' station on the CCEHR which had assumed the name 'Strand' on 9 June 1915, the GNPBR station was renamed 'Aldwych' from the same date. It was closed between September 1940 and June 1946 for use as a public air-raid shelter and permanently on 30 September 1994.

The ticket hall building is one of the few Leslie Green stations which had unconnected façades. One elevation faces onto Strand itself and is the simplest of all Green designs, comprising a single semi-

circular window above the entrance (1). The lettering displaying the names of both station and railway has survived intact, although the former had been hidden from view behind a canopy for around 70 years before being revealed and restored in recent years, while the latter is not in fact in its original form ('TUBE' instead of the existing 'RLY'). The larger façade fronts onto Surrey Street and it too retains early raised lettering (2). However, the first floor level was modified extensively circa 1928, with the arched window being replaced by rectangular versions.

The ticket hall is amongst the most complete of any Green station (3). The original mauve mosaic floor survives, as do some superb tiled signs just inside the Strand entrance, an early ticket office window and one of the timber fronted lifts. The low level passageways and platforms retain much of their original colour scheme, featuring cream and dark green tiling, but in poor condition.

BROMPTON ROAD

2

The station opened on 15 December 1906 as part of the Great Northern Piccadilly & Brompton Railway. It closed permanently on 29 July 1934, although it was later converted for use as a storage and anti-aircraft control facility during World War II.

As at Aldwych, the ticket hall building had two unconnected elevations, facing onto Brompton Road and Cottage Place. The former served as the primary means of access to and egress from the station and was a typical Green design, although it featured an unusual protruding section of cornice at high level (1). This façade was demolished in 1972 to facilitate road widening but the Cottage Place façade still survives (2). Little of the ticket hall itself remains but the platforms are still largely intact behind brick walls and unusually much has not been overpainted, meaning that some of the station name lettering on the wall tiles is still exposed (3).

1

DOWN STREET

The station opened on 15 March 1907 as part of the Great Northern Piccadilly & Brompton Railway. It closed permanently on 21 May 1932, although it was later converted for use as the headquarters of the Railway Executive Committee during World War II.

The building, located on the western side of Down Street 50 metres from its junction with Piccadilly, has a simple, three window façade in largely good condition (1). Nothing of the ticket hall survives but the door to the left of the retail unit gains access to the spiral staircase which leads down to the lower levels of the station. Many of the finishes in this staircase and the corridors leading to the platforms remain intact, while the platforms themselves are still divided into numerous rooms reflecting their wartime function.

EUSTON

The station opened on 22 June 1907 as part of the Charing Cross Euston & Hampstead Railway. The original ticket hall building was closed on 30 September 1914 when improved access was provided from beneath the main line concourse

The building, located on the junction of Drummond Street and Melton Street, occupies a corner site and is similar in appearance to those at Covent Garden and Oxford Circus (1). To the rear may be observed a contemporary sub-station building (2). Little of the ticket hall finishes survive following conversion of the lift shafts for ventilation purposes. However some remain in the access passageways at low level. The CCEHR platforms (now serving the Charing Cross branch of the Northern Line) retained their blue and cream wall tiling until the mid-1980s when it was covered by vitreous enamel metal panels as part of a modernisation project.

SOUTH KENTISH TOWN

The station opened on 22 June 1907 as part of the Charing Cross Euston & Hampstead Railway. It closed permanently on 5 June 1924, although it was later converted for use as a public air-raid shelter during World War II.

The building, located at the junction of Kentish Town Road and Castle Road, has a simple Green façade which is still largely intact although in poor condition (1). Entrance to the ticket hall was previously via the bay beneath the left-hand window, with exit from the lifts via the side elevation, which unusually is lacking the standard faience cladding. Few original finishes may be observed throughout the rest of the station.

1

YORK ROAD

The station was opened as part of the Great Northern Piccadilly & Brompton Railway on 15 December 1906 and closed permanently on 17 September 1932. It was not converted for war-time use unlike many other disused stations.

The building, located on York Road near its junction with Bingfield Street, has a layout similar to that to be found at Hampstead with two façades linked by a third short elevation once containing the entrance (2). Remnants of the gilded raised lettering proclaiming the station name may still be observed. Few original finishes may be observed throughout the rest of the station, having been extensively painted over at low level.

2

ARCHWAY

The station, under the name 'Highgate', opened on 22 June 1907 as one of the two northern termini of the Charing Cross Euston & Hampstead Railway. A second entrance from Highgate Hill was added in 1912. Escalators were brought into service in place of the original lifts in June 1931 and major changes to the ticket hall took place at the same time, including the replacement of both frontages by new designs by Charles Holden. Eight years later, the line was extended to East Finchley and the station name changed to 'Archway (Highgate)' to distinguish it from the new Highgate station being constructed

on the extension. The name was altered to 'Highgate (Archway)' in January 1941 before assuming its current form in December 1947. The ticket hall was completely rebuilt around 1975–77 and now forms the ground level of a tall office block.

Almost all of the station's original features have been lost, with the exception of some wall tiling in the access passageways at platform level, the remainder having been renewed in the mid-1970s.

The original elevation facing Junction Road illustrates many of the key features of Green's work - the decorative cornice, the semi-circular windows covered by hood

moulds extending from prominent pilasters, the raised lettering on a white frieze typical of the CCEHR stations and Maxim arc lamps cantilevered via ornate brackets from the wall (1).

The passageway and staircase leading from the bottom of the spiral staircase to the northern end of the northbound platform are the only areas to have retained their original finishes, although portals to the adjacent tunnel mouth and some cross-passageways have also survived. The dark brown and cream tiling gives an impression of the colour scheme used at platform level, although its extension over the tunnel soffits is a much later addition.

BAKER STREET

The station was opened on 10 March 1906 as the temporary terminus of the Baker Street & Waterloo Railway, although an adjacent station of the same name serving the Metropolitan Railway had opened 43 years previously. A footbridge linking the BSWR ticket hall to the MR platforms was constructed later the same year. Extensive modifications were undertaken in the late 1930s in connection with the opening of a new branch of the Bakerloo Line (as the BSWR had become), including the provision of escalator access to low level.

The original BSWR building, located on the eastern side of Baker Street just to the north of the Lost Property Office, had a typical Green façade, as the photograph from 1933 illustrates (1). However, this was misleading for the ticket hall was not at street level but in fact accessed by means of stair-

cases leading down to the basement. The provision of escalators led to this ticket hall and its lifts being taken out of service in 1940, although it was not until 24 years later that the building was demolished.

Some portals in a passageway close to the northbound Bakerloo Line platform are the only original BSWR features to have survived in public view throughout the remainder of the station. The metal grille covers the entrance to what was once the entry/exit route to the four lifts (2).

CHARING CROSS

The station, under the name 'Trafalgar Square', opened on 10 March 1906 as part of the Baker Street & Waterloo Railway. The BSWR ticket hall was enlarged in 1926 with the opening of escalators in place of lifts. This and Strand station were combined as one called 'Charing Cross' in association with the construction of the Jubilee Line, acting as the line's terminus from May 1979 until the opening of its extension to Stratford 20 years later.

Almost nothing of the stations' original features or finishes remains in public view. Neither had a street level building, with the sub-surface ticket halls being accessed by means of staircases. The ornate iron railings surrounding one of these staircases in Trafalgar Square has survived (1), along with a similar example above a disused staircase on Charing Cross Road opposite the Garrick Theatre.

EARL'S COURT

The station opened on 15 December 1906 on the Great Northern Piccadilly & Brompton Railway, although services on the District Railway had commenced some 35 years earlier. Escalators were installed between the deep level platforms and a new concourse beneath the surface tracks in November 1911 - Earl's Court being the first station in London to be so fitted.

The magnificent frontage facing onto Earl's Court Road was constructed around 1905 and replaced an earlier brick building on the same site. Although designed by the District Railway's chief architect, Harry Ford, there

are distinct similarities with Green's work, notably the arched windows at first floor level and the use of glazed terracotta albeit in a golden-brown hue. Barons Court station shares similar characteristics. The spiral staircase leading to

the Piccadilly Line is accessed directly off one of the sub-surface platforms - a layout unique to this station - and retains its GNPBR wall tiling (2). This, along with the tile bands over the platform soffits, is the only original feature remaining.

EMBANKMENT

The station opened on 10 March 1906 as part of the Baker Street & Waterloo Railway, although services had first served the District Line platforms some 36 years earlier. It was renamed 'Charing Cross (Embankment)' on 6 April 1914 and 'Charing Cross' on 9 May the following year. The station was renamed 'Embankment' on 12 September 1976.

Nothing of the station's original features or finishes remains in public view. As with the nearby stations at Trafalgar Square and Strand, there was no separate street level building. Almost all of the original platform wall tiling (1) has survived but it is covered over by vitreous enamel metal cladding installed during a 1980s station modernisation programme.

GREEN PARK

The station, under the name 'Dover Street', opened on 15 December 1906 on the Great Northern Piccadilly & Brompton Railway. A new ticket hall constructed beneath Piccadilly with escalators accessing the platforms was opened in September 1933 and the station was given its current name from that time.

The original building was located at 5-7 Dover Street on the north side of Piccadilly and was very similar in style and proportion to the façade that survives nearby at Down Street (2). At platform level, the tile bands over the soffits of the Piccadilly Line tunnels and the overbridge leading to the lifts which once served this station are all that survive of the original features in public view.

HOLBORN

The station was opened on 15 December 1906 on the Great Northern Piccadilly & Brompton Railway. Services on the branch line to Strand (later Aldwych) commenced on 30 November the following year. Escalators were installed in place of lifts in the early 1930s, along with the construction of new platforms on the Central Line in order to afford direct interchange between the two railways. The station's name was changed to 'Holborn (Kingsway)' on 22 May 1933, the suffix later dropped.

2

When constructed, the station had two elevations, the more prominent fronting onto Kingsway (1). However unlike all other station buildings on the Yerkes tube railways (with the exception of Golders Green), neither had the standard ox-blood faience cladding. Instead Green made use of a coloured granite (assumed to be red) to complement the high quality architectural finishes adopted for other buildings in the newly opened Kingsway thorough-fare. Both façades – the other being on High Holborn (2) – were replaced in the early 1930s by the Holden elevations that survive now.

Although no traces of original finishes survive on the Piccadilly Line areas of the station, one of the two platforms which served the Aldwych branch when it opened remains largely intact and indicates the distinctive colour scheme and patterning within the tiling used elsewhere (3).

The station, under the name 'King's Cross', opened on 15 December 1906 on the Great Northern Piccadilly & Brompton Railway, although services had first served the Metropolitan Railway platforms almost 44 years earlier. It was renamed 'King's Cross for St Pancras' in 1927 and the entire station assumed its current title six years later.

The original ticket hall building was located near the forecourt of King's Cross main-line station and had perhaps the widest and most unusual of all façades designed by Green (1). Note the unusual arrangement of windows incorporated within this building compared with its counterparts. The inclusion of Venetian windows and arched windows extending up against the cornice are both extremely rare features. The building was made largely redundant when a new circular ticket hall was opened beneath the King's Cross forecourt in June 1939. Although new escalators were provided, two of the lift shafts were retained in service during the period 1948–53. The structure was finally demolished in 1963.

The only original feature to survive in public areas is a lift entrance portal located in a cross-passageway off the eastbound Piccadilly Line platform (2).

KNIGHTSBRIDGE

The station opened on 15 December 1906 on the Great Northern Piccadilly & Brompton Railway. The original building and lifts were replaced on 18 February 1934 by a new sub-surface ticket hall beneath the junction with Sloane Street, with escalators leading down to platform level. A second ticket hall and flight of escalators was opened at the western end of the station on 30 July of the same year. An enlarged ticket hall concourse is currently being constructed beneath the junction of Brompton Road and Hans Crescent, and is due for completion in early 2003.

The ticket hall was originally accessed by means of an arcade linking Brompton Road and Basil Street. The entrance building facing onto the former may at first glance appear to have had a typical Green frontage (1). However upon closer inspection, the presence of several distinctive features are evident, notably the inclusion of ornate floral mouldings, stylised lettering on the white frieze and the open nature of the central arched 'window'. Unfortunately, this unique façade has since been demolished. However, the other entrance to the arcade survives and now forms part of the Basil Hotel (2). Furthermore, some ox-blood faience cladding remains intact on the side wall of Hooper's Court down the side of the Hotel, although it is not totally clear whether this in fact formed part of the station itself (3). None of the original finishes remain visible inside the station. At street level, retail shops now stand on the original site (4).

The station was opened on 10 March 1906 as part of the Baker Street & Waterloo Railway. Platforms serving the Great Northern Piccadilly & Brompton Railway opened on 15 December of the same year. As with several other stations in central London, the street level ticket hall and the lifts leading down to the platforms proved to have inadequate capacity and they were replaced by escalators and a sub-surface ticket hall beneath the Circus itself - the facilities being brought into service on 10 December 1928.

No traces of original finishes survive in public view, following the 1920s reconstruction work and an extensive modernisation project in the late 1980s. However, the original station was unique in that it boasted three separate frontages – fronting onto Piccadilly (1), Haymarket (2) and Jermyn Street (3). The latter is perhaps of most interest because of the ornate stone surrounds to the doorway between the entry and exit bays. Note also the protruding section of cornice, also found on the Piccadilly façade and one of those at Brompton Road amongst others. All three elevations survived as access points to the station until as recently as 1990 when the entire block was redeveloped.

3

TOTTENHAM COURT ROAD

The station, under the name 'Oxford Street', opened on 22 June 1907 on the Charing Cross Euston & Hampstead Railway, although services through an adjacent Central London Railway station called 'Tottenham Court Road' had commenced six years earlier, on 30 July 1900. The CCEHR station changed its name to 'Tottenham Court Road' on 9 March 1908, the CCEHR station of the same name being altered to 'Goodge Street' on the same day so as to avoid confusion. The sub-surface CCEHR ticket hall was enlarged to allow the installation of escalators to serve both sets of platforms, the facilities becoming fully functional by February 1926.

Few traces of the original station survive, following the 1920s reconstruction work and an extensive modernisation project in the mid-1980s. Of those that do, the railings surrounding two of the staircases leading down from street level either side of Tottenham Court Road are the most significant (1). In this view from outside the Dominion Theatre, part of the original CLR station building on the south side of Oxford Street may be observed to the right. The only other remnants of early finishes can be found in the corridor at the base of the spiral staircase which still leads down from ticket hall level (2). Note that tiling survives on both walls and as bands over the soffit, while the portals which once served as access points to and from the lifts may be seen to the left.

WATERLOO

The station was opened on 10 March 1906 as part of the Baker Street & Waterloo Railway, although platforms serving the Waterloo & City Railway had been in operation since 8 August 1898. The station was substantially rebuilt in association with the introduction of Northern Line services, including the provision of a new ticket hall beneath the main line station and a wide concourse between the two sets of platforms – all facilities becoming functional by October 1927. An extra ticket hall was provided on York Road to provide better access to part of the 1951 Festival of Britain exhibition being held nearby, while extensive modifications were undertaken to the ticket hall under the main line station, most recently for the introduction of Channel Tunnel and Jubilee Line services.

Few traces of the original station survive, following the various spells of reconstruction work and an extensive modernisation project in the late 1980s. The original BSWR building was on the eastern side of York Road (1), although it has since been demolished. This simple single storey frontage formed the entrance to a passageway leading to the ticket hall. Note the Underground Electric Railways monograms above the station name.

Imitation Green

AS DESIGN ICONS, Green's stations come close to ranking with the diagrammatic tube map and the Routemaster bus as typifying London and its public transport. In films and on television, his stations have been given more prominence than those of other architects and much shooting takes place on Aldwych's disused platforms, where film crews and actors can work undisturbed. Green's street level buildings are uniquely recognisable as Underground stations because of his use of a standard approach to their design. Although no two Green stations are the same, each is unmistakably an Underground station, even after closure and the removal of all signage. This has led to their use as symbols of the Underground when, perhaps, the Underground organisation would rather been seen in a more modern light.

Probably for this reason, it was a Green style of station building that the producers of the BBC soap opera EastEnders believed would symbolise Walford's position on the Underground network. Walford East station (1) is, presumably, on the District Line to the east of Bow Road, far away from the nearest genuine Green stations on the Bakerloo, Northern and Piccadilly lines. It shares with Golders Green the distinction of a staircase leading up to the platforms, instead of lifts descending to subterranean tubes. The station employs window glazing reminiscent of that in fashion in the 1930s by the main line railways, notably the Great Western, but not looking at all out of place here.

For an exhibition on wartime London, the Smithsonian Institute in Washington chose the basic elements of a Leslie Green station design (2), notably the ox-blood coloured facing bricks and the arch-shaped window.

During extensive restoration work at Gloucester Road station, the architect responsible for the contract, David Wrightson, arranged for photographic images of the façades to be applied to plastic sheeting, which was then applied to boards screening off the building work (3,4). This proved to be a very effective way of maintaining the identity of the station and preventing upheaval to the commercial lettings while the work was carried out. Restoration was completed in 1997.

Cartouche Designs

MANY LESLIE GREEN stations were given decorative touches at first floor level, in addition to the repeat patterns edging some of the window arches. This decoration took the form of cartouches between the arched windows and also on the corners of those buildings with more than one façade.

The most commonly used cartouche design (1) appears on the exteriors of Brompton Road, Caledonian Road, Camden Town, Euston, Hyde Park Corner, Kentish Town, Lambeth North, Leicester Square and Russell Square station buildings. It was also used on the now demolished Dover Street and Warren Street buildings.

Five stations shared another design (2), these being Baker Street, Covent Garden, Oxford Circus and Piccadilly Circus and the now closed York Road.

The other shared design was applied to Belsize Park and Hampstead stations (3).

Individual cartouches were designed for the exteriors of: Chalk Farm (4), Down Street (5), Elephant & Castle (6), Euston (7), Gloucester Road (8), Holloway Road (9, 10), Kings Cross (11), South Kensington (12), South Kentish Town (13), Tufnell Park (14) and York Road (15) stations. See also the LER shield on the corner of Oxford Circus station (illustrated on page 57).

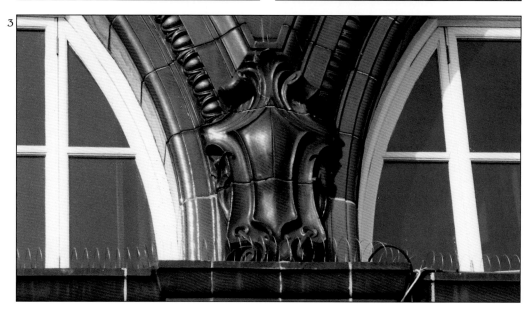

4

5

6

7

8

9

10

11

12

13

14

15

16

17

18

A completely individual design was applied to the exterior of Knightsbridge (16,17), unfortunately no longer existing but thankfully recorded in photographs. At Knightsbridge, art nouveau not only decorated either end of the facade at first floor level and between the window arches, but different designs finished off each end of the station name frieze above the arches (see page 86), the style being strikingly reminiscent of the work of Hector Guimard decorating some Paris Metro station entrances.

The other individual treatment, but in a similar style to the other Green stations, adorned the original Piccadilly Circus street level buildings (18) in Piccadilly and Jermyn Street, at either end of the cornice at roof level.

Not every street level building designed by Leslie Green was decorated with cartouches. Those not so adorned were: Aldwych, Arsenal, Edgware Road, Goodge Street, Highgate (Archway), Marylebone and Mornington Crescent.